Hegel

Three Studies

Hegel

Three Studies

Theodor W. Adorno

translated by Shierry Weber Nicholsen
with an introduction by
Shierry Weber Nicholsen and Jeremy J. Shapiro

The MIT Press, Cambridge, Massachusetts, and
London, England

First MIT Press paperback edition, 1994

This edition © 1993 Massachusetts Institute of Technology
This work originally appeared in German under the title *Drei Studien zu Hegel,*
© 1963, 1971 Suhrkamp Verlag, Frankfurt am Main, Germany.

This book was set in Baskerville by The Maple-Vail Book Manufacturing
Group and was printed and bound in the United States of America.

Library of Congress Cataloging-in-Publication Data
Adorno, Theodor W., 1903-1969.
  [Drei Studien zu Hegel. English]
  Hegel : three studies / Theodor W. Adorno ; translated by Shierry
  Weber Nicholsen ; with an introduction by Shierry Weber Nicholsen
  and Jeremy J. Shapiro.
    p. cm.—(Studies in contemporary German social thought)
  Translation of: Drei Studien zu Hegel.
  Includes bibliographical references and index.
  ISBN 0-262-01131-X (HB), 0-262-51080-4 (PB)
  1. Hegel, Georg Wilhelm Friedrich, 1770-1831. I. Title.
II. Series.
B2948.A3213   1993
193—dc20   92-23161
                                                       CIP

For Karl Heinz Haag

Contents

Introduction

Shierry Weber Nicholsen
Jeremy J. Shapiro

I salute you from the Petrified Forest of human culture
Where nothing is left standing
But where roam great swirling lights
Which call for the deliverance of foliage and bird.
From your fingers flows the sap of trees in flower.

André Breton, Ode to Charles Fourier

The development of critical philosophy and social theory in the twentieth century, especially that of Theodor W. Adorno and the Frankfurt School, has been intimately linked with the appropriation and reinterpretation of the thinkers of German Idealism, most notably Hegel. Such thinkers as Adorno, Max Horkheimer, Herbert Marcuse, and Jürgen Habermas, through a critical hermeneutic dialogue with Kant, Schiller, Schelling, Hegel, Schopenhauer, Marx, Kierkegaard, and Nietzsche, elaborated their own theoretical oeuvre and reinterpreted the trends and contradictions of the present historical period through the perspective provided by these nineteenth-century philosophers. At the same time, they made important contributions to our understanding of these thinkers. To do so, they had to pry the earlier philosophers' thought out of traditional academic, dogmatic, and ideological interpretations in order to unfold the core concepts and critique contained in their work. This hermeneutic was continuously elaborated as part of a radical political, cultural, and social critique of advanced capitalism and authoritarian political tendencies. It was undertaken with the explicit conviction that positivistic and one-dimensional thinking was inherent in the apparatus of domination in advanced industrial society and that the major nineteenth-century German philosophers, especially in their critique of narrow Enlightenment and positivist thinking, could help lay the foundations for a new critical relationship to advanced industrial society. It is quite characteristic that the earliest works of the major thinkers of the Frankfurt School (if we include their doctoral dissertations and *Habilitationsschriften*) include major studies of Kant, Schiller, Schelling, Hegel, and Kierkegaard, and that their later works include studies of Hegel, Marx, Schopenhauer, and Nietzsche, as well as of Freud and Max Weber, whom the critical theorists saw as the bridge between the philosophical tradition and the social sciences. In addition, they analyzed major twentieth-century thinkers, including Husserl, Heidegger, Sartre, Dewey, Carnap, and Wittgenstein, as philosopher-ideologists.

The core of the critical theorists' approach is the immanent critique of ideology. Truth is attained by unfolding both the truth content and the contradictions of thought through linking it to the truth content and contradictions of its social context and commitments. This leads to a historically relativized truth that is maximally universal precisely through awareness of its historical and social situation and limitations. The critique of ideology means taking theory at its word and at its deed. Hence the Frankfurt School produced an imposing series of critical hermeneutic studies of social theory and philosophy, most of which are important both as philosophical and sociological works in their own right and as valuable contributions to the understanding of other theorists.[1] No other thinker was as important to this critical hermeneutics as Hegel. The critical theorists aimed at a dialectical method that was not embroiled in the vagaries of socialist party politics and positivistic or metaphysical interpretations of Marx. In both Hegel and Marx, the dialectical method claimed to provide a unity of theoretical and practical reason that seemed torn asunder in contemporary civilization and philosophy. And the systematic character of Hegel's thinking promised a possible unification of the human sciences that the critical theorists sought to bring about for the radical understanding of contemporary society through the integration of sociology, psychology, economics, political science, and philosophy. Hegel's own critique of the limitations of the scientific worldview on the one hand and its romantic alternative on the other—an intellectual situation that in some ways parallels that of the juxtaposition of twentieth-century positivism and pragmatism on the one hand and phenomenology, existentialism, and hermeneutics on the other—suggested an analogous critique of these contemporary schools of thought. Hegel claimed, and intended, to be the culmination of Western rationalism, and this made his thought an appropriate focus for the critique of Western civilization. Above all, Hegel's focus on the negative and the power of negation and contradiction inherent in thought and reality seemed a key to rescuing the negative from the overwhelming affirmative power of advanced industrial society.

Adorno, and Marcuse as well, regarded Hegel, despite his obvious conservative tendencies, as the true revolutionary thinker—perhaps more so than Marx—if the negative and dialectical core of this thought could be rescued from its embeddedness in a doctrine of undialectical affirmation, reconciliation, and unification. Marcuse, in *Reason and Revolution,* published a half-century ago, attempted to articulate the negative, critical, and dialectical core of Hegel's thought and to preserve it in a properly understood Marxism: a Marxism that synthesizes the humanistic core of Marx's early writings, the historical materialism of the *German Ideology*, and the dialectical analysis contained in Marx's mature economic theory. Marcuse, skeptical of the revolutionary potential of either social democracy or Leninist communism, nevertheless saw in Hegel a dialectical method that could be the basis for a socialism appropriate to the historical situation of advanced industrial society. Published during World War II, *Reason and Revolution* looked toward this humanistically and dialectically regenerated Marxism as a historical possibility after the defeat of Nazism. Adorno, writing after World War II and the stabilization of the domination structure of advanced industrial society following the defeat of Nazism, and after his and Max Horkheimer's *Dialectic of Enlightenment*, which focuses on capitalist industrialism's ability to eliminate all opposition to the domination of both internal and external nature, sought to recuperate in Hegel the basis for a dialectic of resistance to that power of domination by concentrating on the nonidentical, that which is beyond the domination of reason.

In their interpretations of Hegel, both Marcuse and Adorno attempt to provide a philosophical basis for "negative thinking": for thought that desires to free itself from the shackles of the "logos of domination" and to serve as a basis for and interpretation of emancipation in the broadest historical sense—emancipation from class domination, from the "iron cage" of bureaucratic rationality, from the terror world of the concentration camp, from the "performance principle," and from one-dimensional thought, administered culture, and deformed experience. Over the half century since the publication of Marcuse's *Reason and Revolution*, and despite ongoing emancipatory undercurrents and outbreaks of emancipatory movements, the ability of the universal market society, combined with powerful state formations, to control or absorb opposition and cut off alternatives appears to have increased. But as Adorno says in "Aspects of Hegel's Philosophy,"

a world integrated through "production," through the exchange relationship, depends in all its moments on the social conditions of its production, and in that sense actually realizes the primacy of the whole over its parts; in this regard the desperate impotence of every single individual now verifies Hegel's extravagant conception of the system. . . . The self-forgetfulness of production, the insatiable and destructive expansive principle of the exchange society, is reflected in Hegelian metaphysics. It describes the way the world actually is, not in historical perspective but in essence.

This continuity in "the way the world actually is" calls for renewed negative or dialectical thinking, and hence for a renewed understanding of Hegel, who was its founder in an emphatic sense. And this method of thought and analysis cannot be simply an opposition or negation from the outside. Rather, to use the concept that both Marcuse and Adorno identified as central to Hegel, it must be "determinate negation," negation that emerges out of and is specific to what it negates, and that is part of its very essence. That is why negative thinking, or dialectical thinking, is both a method and not a method.

Prior to recent currents of antifoundationalism, all of modern philosophy was marked by a struggle for method. This impetus extends from Descartes's *Discourse* through Kant's *Critique,* Hegel's *Phenomenology* and *Logic,* and Marx's *German Ideology* to Husserl's *Ideas* and the writings of the early Wittgenstein and Carnap. The priority of method is intimately linked with the idea of the subject—epistemological method, logical foundation, and the grounding of knowledge and truth in the subject are part of a single historical project. Even the critique of the bourgeois notion of the subject in Marx and critical theory is carried out in the interest of a less restrictive, less repressive, and less repressed subject. Since Lukács's announcement, in *History and Class Consciousness,* that orthodoxy in Marxism is a matter of method rather than of content, the development of Marxian social theory has been bound up with the question of the nature of this method and the related question of the historical subject. The critical theorists of the Frankfurt School, in particular, were preoccupied with this question, in the light of the lapsing of the revolutionary working class as a historical subject. Whereas Lukács identified the subject with the working class and the Communist party, the critical theorists' economic, sociological, and cultural analysis, combined with the course of political events, could not support this identification. Hence neither Marcuse nor Adorno could any longer "transcend" Hegel, as Marx had, by projecting Hegel's categories onto social categories (although Marcuse continued to be concerned with the question of an emergent historical subject). To the contrary, critical theory returned to Hegel partly out of the bankruptcy of precisely this Marxian "overcoming" and projection of Hegel.

Adorno's thought in general, and his interpretation of Hegel in particular, sets itself an ironic task: that of developing a dialectical method, with its connections to a self-reflective subject, in a context defined as one in which the subject has been liquidated by its own attempt to liquidate everything outside of itself. And his dialectical thought cannot merely attempt to resurrect the liquidated subject. For a true, negative dialectic must strive to attain precisely that otherness that is denied by a subject-oriented dialectic. That is why Adorno differentiates himself from Hegel most emphatically in relation to the concepts of identity and nonidentity. In a telling and paradoxical formulation that fully expresses German Idealism's attempt to reduce everything to subjectness, Hegel argued for the identity of identity and nonidentity. Even that which is most resistant to, or outside, the subject and the concept is conceived as a moment of an underlying unity that is itself subject and concept, thus converting recognition of the limitation of rationality into a hidden affirmation of it. Adorno's own approach to "standing Hegel on his head" was to argue precisely for the "nonidentity of identity and nonidentity": subjectness and mind, in those very accomplishments in which they have most recognized what is beyond or outside them, must strain toward one further dimension of the "beyondness" of this "beyond," recognizing that it is really beyond—yet without thereby reducing themselves to slavish heteronomy or self-effacement.

Hence Adorno's insistence on the experiential content of Hegel's philosophy and on the imperative that a dialectical philosophy immerse itself in the experience of the object. That is why, for Adorno, the dialectical method cannot be reduced to a set of axioms or formulas. Method in that sense is inherently subjectivistic, in that it presumes that reality conveniently arranges itself in accordance with the postulates and preferences of thought. If dialectical thinking is to avoid this idealistic presumption (which can easily take on a materialistic form, as in "dialectical materialism"), then it must shape itself to the contours of the object—not as an irreducible given but as something with its own tensions and contradictions, which include those of the thought that tries to comprehend it. This approach holds equally for the understanding of Hegel's own thought, looking for its truth both in what it grasps and in what it conceals, in what it points to beyond itself as well as in what keeps it from grasping that to which it points, in what it says as well as in what it tries to say but cannot.

Adorno's *Hegel* is not merely a lesson in negative thinking. It is also, like all his work, a lesson in negative experience. His method is an indissoluble unity of thinking and experiencing: this is the unifying thread that runs through all his work, from *Negative Dialectics* and these essays on Hegel through his analyses of musical and literary works to his personal reflections and aphorisms. This is perhaps what most distinguishes Adorno's critical theory from other currents of neo-Marxian theory. Not only should it not be understood as mere theory, it is not an attempt (however flawed) at a unity of theory and practice. Rather, it intends to be an ensemble that integrates theory, the orientation of practice, and experience and sensibility. Indeed, Adorno's work, along with that of Benjamin, is in part an argument that the notion of theory, practice, and their unity, as found in the Marxian tradition, is defective—precisely because of and to the extent of its neglect of experience. It is this aspect of his work that is most radical and, to some, indigestible.

Adorno's work is thus a model of a particular way of experiencing the world. It is an explicit and implicit argument that negative experience is the authentic form of experience for those who live in a contradictory, antagonistic society, an upside-down, perverted world. That is why Adorno's intention in *Hegel* and his other work is in large part the preservation, development, and transmission of a specific relation to experience, which relates to what is by relating to what is not, and relates to what is not by relating to what is. And it is because Hegelian philosophy is the first articulation of the saturation of experience with negativity that Adorno asserts that "these days it is hardly possible for a theoretical idea of any scope to do justice to the experience of consciousness, and in fact not only the experience of consciousness but the bodily experience of the human being, without having incorporated something of Hegel's philosophy." ("Aspects")

Introduction

For an individual living in a contradictory, perverted society, dialectical experience is an essential vehicle for the preservation not only of the truth—the cognitive truth about that society—but of his or her own identity. That is why negative experience is an experience not only of negation but also of affirmation. It is true that much of the modern experience of the perverted world takes the form of immediate negation, of nausea, shock, alienation, dissonance, and despair. But while the expression of this negation is a part of the truth, it is only a partially developed form of it. For the real truth about reality includes awareness of the potentiality, the desire, and the justification for transcending the perverted world. It must go beyond the merely dialectical to what Hegel calls the speculative, in which the antagonisms of the dialectic are resolved. The individual in advanced capitalist society, who recognizes that nothing within that society escapes contamination by domination and the commodity principle, can maintain a true identity only through the negation of all the givens of the surrounding society and culture. Such an existence is governed by orientation to the truth. It relates, through dialectical thought, practice, and experience, to the essence of things. But through this relation, it discerns and experiences the good, the true, and the beautiful through their deformations—as the negation of the latter, and as real in this negation. It pursues freedom and happiness in a repressive and oppressive society without ideologically denying this repression and oppression. It pursues the life of a critical intellect without suffering the deformation and rigidifcation of experience that is the normal form of intellectual life in capitalist society.

Both Marcuse's *Reason and Revolution* and Adorno's *Hegel: Three Studies* are works of the critical theorists as teachers who want to pass on to actual or potential students the tools of thought that will enable them to carry out the difficult tasks involved in the critical analysis of the world and of thought. Marcuse and Adorno are teachers not as expounders of doctrine, however, but as interpreters of texts that are among the most difficult and contradictory of modern thought: texts that, despite their emphasis on reason, appear hermetic and, as Adorno states, occasionally undecipherable. In both works one detects the pathos of teachers who are concerned lest rare and precious tools that can accomplish marvels fall into disuse such that future generations may no longer be able to match their ancestors' achievements, the way perhaps late-Roman literati may have viewed the tradition of rhetoric, or the way craftspeople may look at the specialized knowledge that is lost in mass production and automation.

Thus while *Hegel: Three Studies* is certainly a work of Hegel scholarship and interpretation, it is also a work of pedagogy. Of Adorno's writings it is perhaps the closest to representing the intellectual atmosphere and style of working of Adorno's *Philosophisches Hauptseminar* (Philosophy Seminar) at the Johann Wolfgang Goethe University in Frankfurt during the last decade of Adorno's life, when he had become one of postwar Germany's philosophical luminaries and influential teachers. The Philosophisches Hauptseminar was given every semester and was devoted almost exclusively to the primary works of Kant and Hegel. It was in these seminars—as well as in related lectures at the University—that Adorno philosophically elaborated the negative dialectics of his later thought. These seminars and lectures were a primary influence on the intellectual leaders of the German New Left. A frequently told student joke in Frankfurt went, "The Revolution is breaking out on the street? Too bad—I can't miss Adorno's lecture."

The features of Adorno's philosophical seminars that stand out in recollection figure prominently in the Hegel essays as well. The first was a dialogue among three participants: Kant, Hegel, and Adorno (and Max Horkheimer when he was still participating in the seminar), in which Adorno attempted to bring out both the relative truth content and the relative limitation of Kant and Hegel in relation to one another, against the background of Marxian, materialist assumptions. Adorno vindicated both Hegel's argument against Kant—that the limitations of reason set by Kant already implied the transcendence of these limits—and Kant's argument for the necessity of something outside the totalizing tendency of thought. The second was the centrality of the Hegelian category of mediation to every aspect of dialectical thinking. Most of the philosophical currents and schools of thought of both Hegel's day and our own posit, as absolutes or irreducible givens, principles or entities that are in fact the results of abstraction or moments in processes outside themselves that they do not take into account—the ladder that they have climbed up and thrown away, to use Wittgenstein's phrase. The aim of dialectical thinking is to think not abstractly but *concretely*, by understanding ideas and realities in the contradictions of their specific contexts and processes rather than in "abstraction" from these contexts and processes—to put the ladder back into the thought. And for the critical theorists the relevant contexts and processes are social, cultural, psychological, and intellectual—they are historical through and through. In the seminars the study of Kant and Hegel was carried out in this very way, through meticulous dialectical *explication de texte,* of which the essay "Skoteinos" gives some examples. And typically the semester-long seminar devoted, for example, to Hegel's *Phenomenology of Mind* would have arrived at the eighth or tenth page by the end of the term—with a sense of exhausted achievement, and ready for a different work the following term.

Not only did the critical theorists endeavor to find the truth content of the philosophical tradition through a critical comprehension of it that takes account of its enmeshment in a concrete history that is the history of conflicts about domination, emancipation, reason, freedom, happiness, work, terror, and utopian strivings. They wanted, also, to learn and teach *how to read and understand* the philosophical tradition itself. The first generation of Frankfurt School critical theorists stood in a far different relation to the philosophical tradition of German Idealism than do those who are first encountering it today. In many ways, Marcuse's and Adorno's intellectual environment and training were as close to those of Kant and Hegel as to those of the present. Yet both taught works of Kant and Hegel in the universities, across great historical chasms: Marcuse taught Hegel to students in America in a philosophically alien environment, and Adorno taught to a generation of German students distanced from his own by the Third Reich. We hope that this publication in English of Adorno's Hegel essays, in the last decade of the century, will contribute to the perpetuation and elaboration of dialectical thinking and experience across yet another historical divide.

Rescuing Hegel—and only rescue, not revival, is appropriate for him—means facing up to his philosophy where it is most painful and wresting truth from it where its untruth is obvious.
"The Experiential Content of Hegel's Philosophy"

Adorno's *Hegel: Three Studies* takes the form of an extreme and provocative defense of the truth content in Hegel's philosophy. Writing in the late 1950s and early 1960s, Adorno defends Hegel not only against the dismissals and distortions then current—the positivist's dismissal of him as unintelligible or the Soviet Marxist's ideological version of the dialectic—but also against the liberal's lukewarm homage to Hegel's sense of historical reality. Certainly those views of Hegel persist. But today Adorno's presentation of Hegel is startling even within the context of the contemporary wave of interest in Hegel initiated by the Frankfurt School's own popularity in this country and then reinforced by the French via deconstruction. Adorno's *Hegel* reminds us that now as much as in 1956, when the first of these essays was given as a lecture, it is not a question of what is living and what is dead in Hegel—the question with which Croce initiated the twentieth-century Hegel revival—but a question of "what the present means in the face of Hegel." Adorno presents a Hegel read against the grain and from the perspective of a critique of philosophy as an isolated discipline, but a Hegel who is still, he argues, unsurpassed by any twentieth-century philosophy. The Frankfurt School's critical theory of society represented in some respects a return to Hegel from Marx, and in some respects Adorno's *Hegel* serves to articulate Adorno's own philosophical enterprise as well. Just as Hegel's philosophy attempts to bring to self-consciousness the labors of spirit up to his time, so Adorno's work is a self-reflection of that in Hegel which had not been brought to consciousness within Hegel's own work. In this respect as well, *Hegel* serves as a defense of the contemporary relevance of Adorno and the Frankfurt School.

The aim of *Hegel: Three Studies*, Adorno tells us in his preface, is to prepare "a new conception of the dialectic." The dialectic works through immanent criticism, and this is the approach Adorno takes in his defense of Hegel. It is through immanent criticism that Adorno attacks the truth claims of the various schools of thought—positivism, Gestalt psychology, phenomenology, existential ontology, dialectical materialism—that claim to have surpassed Hegel. More important, Hegel himself, through immanent criticism, will lead thought to that new conception of the dialectic, the "negative dialectics" Adorno expounded in the work of that name published shortly after *Hegel*. The negative dialectic is won by "wresting," as Adorno says, the truth content from

Hegel's philosophy precisely where its untruth is most obvious. Accordingly, it is to the "skandalon" of Hegel's philosophy—its speculative absolute idealism, that which is most faded, most discredited, most outmoded in it, even a sort of philosophical kitsch— that Adorno turns to find a dialectic that makes room for the contingent, the particular, the nonidentical. Speculation is not, Adorno tells us, some kind of "troublesome ornamentation"; on the contrary, Hegel's "substantive insights . . . are produced by speculation":

> Because of his idealism, Hegel has been reproached with being abstract in comparison with the concreteness of the phenomenological, anthropological, and ontological schools. But he brought infinitely more concreteness into this philosophical idea than those approaches, and not because his speculative imagination was balanced by a sense of reality but by virtue of the approach his philosophy takes—by virtue, one might say, of the experiential character of his speculation itself. ("Experiential Content")

How can this be so? One of Adorno's answers is that the dialectic in absolute idealism is conceived nonhierarchically. It is neither a middle between extremes nor a subsumption of the component part under a synthetic whole (for this reason too, the dialectic is not a method nor is Hegel's work a system). Truth emerges from a dialectical interplay of subject and object, of particular and whole, of mediated and unmediated. Although there is no such thing as the pure given or immediate, the pure empirical datum, to serve as a starting point—an error that, as Adorno points out, both empiricism and its irrationalist critics make—a subject conceived in opposition to empirical reality is also impossible, a mere empty subjectivism. All interpretations of Hegel that end by dismissing him fail to accommodate this nonhierarchical conception of the dialectic. If truth is process in this sense, it is also concrete. The movement of thought is powered by the self-reflection of the subject attempting to conceive reality, and ultimately the absoluteness of idealism obliterates the distinction between subject and object: "If, as in Hegel, in the totality everything ultimately collapses into the subject as absolute spirit, idealism thereby cancels itself out, because no difference remains through which the subject could be identified as something distinct, as subject," ("Experiential Content"). Still, Hegel had attempted to formulate the dialectic and the subject-object as absolute subject. Hence the nonsubsumability of the particular becomes apparent at the same time Hegel's philosophy denies it. Hegel's philosophy is thus self-contradictory by its own criterion, and it is the criterion, the dialectic, that Adorno holds out, against Hegel, as the bearer of the truth content.

Another of Adorno's answers to the question of how speculation can itself be the experiential content of Hegel's philosophy and can accommodate concreteness takes the form of his development of Hegel's notion of the "*Arbeit des Begriffs*," the labor of the concept. The labor of the spirit—the struggles of truth in process, the exertions of intellectual activity, the efforts involved in wresting Hegel's truth from his untruth—is a form of labor in itself. It is also, Adorno indicates, social labor presented in the guise of logic, and Hegel's absolute spirit is none other than society: "The mystery behind synthetic apperception . . . is none other than social labor" ("Aspects"). While this answer might easily be seen as "sociologism," a neo-Marxist standing of Hegel on his head, Adorno rescues it and gives it a further twist. In a tour de force through which he wrests truth even from Hegel's most notorious work, with its most notorious thesis—the *Philosophy of Right* and its notion that what is real is rational—Adorno develops the notion of antagonistic totality. The ultimate truth of what is most patently false and ideological in Hegel—his equation of reason with reality and in particular with the state—is that, as history has shown, reality has become precisely the kind of system and totality Hegel proposed it to be.[2] It is an antagonistic totality, a totality only by virtue of its contradictions, and a system in which the individual is everywhere governed by the invisible totalizing "web of guilt" that is the persistence of unreason. In this light, Hegel's philosophy becomes critical not only of the details but of the negative whole:

Hegel's philosophy is indeed essentially negative: critique. In extending the transcendental philosophy of the *Critique of Pure Reason* through the thesis of reason's identity with what exists and making it a critique of what exists, a critique of any and every positivity, Hegel denounced the world, whose theodicy constitutes his program, in its totality as well; he denounced it as a web of guilt *[Schuldzusammenhang]* in which, as Mephistopheles says in *Faust,* everything that exists deserves to perish. ("Aspects")

The distinction between labor and nature, between producers and owners, is what produces society as antagonistic totality. Adorno's notion turns on the idea that labor itself has, in this sense, an oppressive aspect, that it is not—and here Adorno takes issue with Marx's celebrated critique of Hegel—the sole producer of value. If Hegel presented a false reconciliation in the *Philosophy of Right,* Hegel's philosophy, in at least aiming toward a genuinely reconciled whole, contains a moment of utopian hope that is elsewhere lost: "The ray of light that reveals the whole to be untrue in all its moments is none other than utopia, the utopia of the whole truth, which is still to be realized" ("Experiential Content").

The notion of spirit's labor is in fact the key to Adorno's interpretation of Hegel and his defense of Hegel's truth. Spirit's labor is the dialectical motor, the reflection of each state of consciousness in its limitation, that forces philosophy to become concrete and ends by permeating, as Adorno says, the idea of totality with the idea of contradiction. And it is that labor that leads philosophy out of its abstract separation from empirical reality and the contingent: "In the *Phenomenology of Spirit,* taking as his critical point of departure what is closest to hand, unmediated human consciousness, [Hegel] accomplishes the mediation of that consciousness in and through the historical movement of what exists, a movement that takes it beyond all mere metaphysics of being. Once set in motion, the concretization of philosophy cannot be stopped for the sake of philosophy's illusory dignity" ("Experiential Content"). Labor, the theme of Adorno's immanent criticism of Hegel, is also the theme of "Skoteinos," the third of his three essays on Hegel. "Skoteinos"—the title alludes to Adorno's defense of the "obscure" Heraclites as opposed to the "clear" Descartes—has an explicitly pedagogical aim. It draws, as Adorno tells us in his preface, directly on his experience teaching Hegel at the University in Frankfurt and is a kind of prolegomenon to reading Hegel—not a reading of Hegel so much as a discussion of what is involved in that reading. The issue in reading Hegel, as Hegel himself had pointed out in the preface to the *Phenomenology,* which serves in its way as a model for "Skoteinos," is that intelligibility (for Adorno, clarity) is not readily attained by true philosophy. The question is what to make of Hegel's lack of clarity, how to understand the truth content of that very unclarity. The complementary question is how to read Hegel productively, in the way that truth content requires, so that the labors that have gone into the writing, and must go into the reading, of Hegel's philosophy are not in vain.

Adorno uses the difficulties of reading Hegel—that at times it is impossible to decipher a passage, that Hegel was not careful in his use of language, that he often made assertions without actually following through on the argumentation, and so on—to point up a problem that goes far beyond any empirical or sub-

jective weakness on Hegel's part. For the difficulties in understanding Hegel are objective, and they derive primarily from the
nature of thought and its relation to language. Hence much of
"Skoteinos" is an attack on the desideratum of clarity as we find
it in Descartes. The demand for clarity presupposes that the object of thought has been tacitly preformed to allow the correspondence of thought and its object. If Hegel's texts differ from
traditional philosophical texts, which at least make a pretense of
logical exposition that is clear at every point, it is in an effort to
do justice to a matter that by its very nature evades this kind of
clarity; philosophy, in Adorno's formulation, is "faced with a
paradox: to say clearly something that is unclear, that has no
firm outline, that does not accommodate to reification." The dialectic to which philosophy must submit in this attempt is the
dialectic of language itself, which has both an expressive and a
communicative element. The communicative aspect, which cannot be renounced, can never be fully adequate to a dialectical
truth, and Adorno defends Hegel's texts on this basis:

In Hegel nothing can be understood in isolation, everything is to be
understood only in the context of the whole, with the awkward qualification that the whole in turn lives only in the individual moments. In
actuality, however, this kind of doubleness of the dialectic eludes literary presentation, which is of necessity finite when it unequivocally states
something equivocal. This is why one has to make so many allowances
for it in Hegel. That it cannot in principle achieve the unity of the whole
and its parts at one blow becomes its weak spot. Every single sentence
in Hegel's philosophy proves itself unsuitable for that philosophy, and
the form expresses this in its inability to grasp any content with complete adequacy. ("Skoteinos")

As a consequence of these dialectics, Hegel's works, with their
equivocations, their lack of consistent argumentation, and their
lack of full editing by their author, become "antitexts"—"if

pressed, one may regard the *Phenomenology* as a book; with the *Science of Logic* this is no longer possible," says Adorno—representing by their very form a critique of a falsely harmonious notion of presentation:

> That a thought that made such extravagant claims should have foregone transmission in specific, definitive form can be explained only in terms of its ideal of presentation, the negation of presentation. At the same time, in the looseness of a delivery that even when most highly elaborated is more spoken than written, one can look for a corrective to the hubris of the conclusive and definitive of which Hegel's work was accused even during his lifetime. ("Skoteinos")

In illuminating the concept of the nonidentical within Hegel's work, Adorno tacitly explicates and justifies his own dialectical-critical method and his own commitment to the nonidentical. He illuminates those aspects of Hegel that most resemble his own thought and from which he has learned the most. Adorno's defense of Hegel's texts in "Skoteinos" echoes his discussion of the essay form and his critique of the Cartesian notion of clarity in "The Essay as Form," the lead essay in his *Notes to Literature,* which dates from the same period as the first of his Hegel essays. *Hegel: Three Studies* as a whole, in fact, is roughly contemporaneous with the majority of the essays collected in Adorno's *Notes to Literature,* the period immediately preceding and overlapping with the production of his last, larger-scale works, *Negative Dialectics* and *Aesthetic Theory.* Adorno's discussion of the demands Hegel's texts make upon the reader reveals in still greater richness the kinship between Adorno and Hegel. Adorno's essayistic work on literary and musical texts and aesthetic issues is formulated in terms of the same dialectic of thought and language we see in "Skoteinos." In that body of work—the essay "Presuppositions," in the second volume of *Notes to Literature,* is a good example—Adorno elaborates a conception of the critical recipient's stance toward aesthetic or intellectual objects, or *geistige Gebilde*. It is a stance characterized by the search for intelligibility as opposed to a strict understanding based on clarity, just as Adorno proposes for the reader of Hegel. What Adorno says about reading Hegel is in fact quite close to what he says in other contexts about the experiential activity of the subject of aesthetic experience:

No doubt Hegel's style goes against customary philosophical understanding, yet in his weaknesses he paves the way for a different kind of understanding; one must read Hegel by describing along with him the curves of his intellectual movement, by playing his ideas with the speculative ear as though they were musical notes. Philosophy as a whole is allied with art in wanting to rescue, in the medium of the concept, the mimesis that the concept represses. ("Skoteinos")

Reading with the speculative ear—the phrase derives originally from Kierkegaard—is a formulation for a kind of aesthetic "participatory following through," or *Mitvollzug,* that demands a dual activity on the part of the reader. On the one hand, the reader must engage in a kind of contemplative passivity—Adorno uses the phenomenological term "spontaneous receptivity"—in which she simply floats along, using what seems to be the intention of the whole as a guide to understanding. This corresponds to the "simply looking on" or *"reines Zusehen,"* of the introduction to Hegel's *Phenomenology,* which Adorno invokes repeatedly. At the same time, the reader's activity is one of immersion in the precise wording, a kind of self-forgetful immersion in details in which, paradoxically, the reader's subjective associations, which are subsequently checked against the text, are of the utmost importance: "Hegel has to be read against the grain, and in such a way that every logical operation, however formal it seems to be, is reduced to its experiential core. The equivalent of such experience in the reader is the imagination. . . . The content itself contains, as a law of its form, the expectation of productive imagination on the part of the one reading" ("Skoteinos").

This kind of imaginative activity, common to both philosophy and art, is the counterpart both of spirit's mimetic labors and of the equivocations within the work that reflect language's dual nature. Spontaneous receptivity requires an openness to the dialectical processes inherent in the object—the "labor of the concept" is both the labor inherent in thought, which is by nature dialectical, and the labor inherent in following an object that is by nature dialectical. Thought imitates the dialectical nonidentity of reality, in which the subject participates. Language, which in its communicative aspect participates in the clarity of conceptual logic, also participates in the mimesis of the nonidentical. The word that Adorno uses as a virtual figure for this mimesis appears in the epigraph for "Skoteinos" as well: "Ich habe nichts als Rauschen," a line from the poet Rudolf Borchardt, for a selection of whose work Adorno later published an introduction, now found in the second volume of *Notes to Literature*. *Rauschen* (which also, as *Rausch,* means ecstasy or intoxication) is the word used for the murmuring of a rushing brook or the rustling of the wind in the trees or the surging of waves on a beach. It refers to language's sensuous aspect and beyond that to the way in which language's intelligible but indistinct activity—what Adorno elsewhere calls "logicity"—imitates the movement of concrete nonidentical reality.

The intimate mimetic relationship between the nonidentical and the labor of spirit is embodied in the most poignant moment of Adorno's *Hegel,* a moment that is also a tour de force: Adorno's defense of Hegel against the charge of being the ultimate bourgeois philosopher and his simultaneous justification of the bourgeois soberness in Hegel, a defense and a justification that, like Adorno's critique of the notion of clarity, is also Adorno's self-defense through the medium of Hegel. Adorno evokes what is most contingent and most nonidentical: Hegel in the flesh, speaking; Hegel with his Swabian dialect and his plain bourgeois face. But what is most contingent and most nonidentical, the person of Hegel, is also the locus of the interplay of spirit and flesh, the locus of the individual exertions required for the life of the spirit, exertions that are at the same time a deliberate divestiture of the self. This notion of the divested self is the altered concept of experience that takes the place of what we think of as "subjective experience."

In evoking the speaking person of Hegel, Adorno practices his own self-divestiture. It is unusual for him to cite anyone but Hegel in the book, but here he gives the floor, at length, to H. G. Hotho, who heard Hegel lecture in Berlin and who describes him as follows (here in Walter Kaufmann's rendering):

Exhausted, morose, he sat there as if collapsed into himself, his head bent down, and while speaking kept turning pages and searching in his long folio notebooks, forward and backward, high and low. His constant clearing of his throat and coughing interrupted any flow of speech. Every sentence stood alone and came out with effort, cut in pieces and jumbled. Every word, every syllable detached itself only reluctantly to receive a strangely thorough emphasis from the metallic-empty voice with its broad Swabian dialect. ("Skoteinos")

What one sees here in the contingent, mortal, fleshly human being is in fact the activity of spirit itself within the individual consciousness: it is thought in action we are seeing. Hotho speaks again:

He faltered even in the beginning, tried to go on, started once more, stopped again, spoke and pondered; the right word seemed to be missing forever, but then it scored most surely. . . . Now one had grasped the clear meaning of a sentence and hoped most ardently to progress. In vain. Instead of moving forward, the thought kept revolving around

the same point with similar words. . . . Slowly and deliberately, making
use of seemingly insignificant links, some full thought . . . limited itself
to the point of one-sidedness. . . . split itself into distinctions and involved itself in contradictions whose victorious solution eventually found
the strength to compel the reunification of the most recalcitrant elements. Thus always taking up again carefully what had gone before in
order to develop out of it more profoundly in a different form what
came later, . . . the most wonderful stream of thought twisted and pressed
and struggled. ("Skoteinos")

In this sense what we think of as subjective experience is in fact
the opposite, a personhood utterly devoted to the objectivity of
its work. By all the subjective means available to it, the philosopher's self effaces itself in the truth of its object. In no sense does
Adorno's evocation of the person of Hegel represent a bio-
graphical interpretation of his thought; rather than the thought
expressing the man, the life of the man himself becomes the life
of spirit: "Like the subject of his theories, the man Hegel had
absorbed both subject and object into himself in spirit; the life
of his spirit is all of life again within itself" ("Aspects"). We may
think of Hegel as having an "intellectual body," says Adorno,
and his philosophy too "*rauscht*"; it murmurs and rustles in mimesis of the nonidentical. It is in this sense that Hegel's philosophy is an expression of experience; philosophy is the expression
of spirit, which is the negation of self in the matter at hand.

It is important that this not be understood as simply a matter
of sublimation or self-transcendence; the element of labor, exertion, and its relation to mortality is clearly present. Self-divestiture in the activity of spirit is akin to death; the life of the spirit
has a kinship with mortality and death. In Adorno's words,
"Hegel's demeanor, full of suffering, his countenance ravaged
by thought, the face of one who has literally consumed himself until he is no more than ashes, bear witness to this self-
divestiture" ("Aspects"). If experience is the core of Hegel's phi-

losophy, then, it is both the distilled experience of life and the experience of thought at work with all its strains and contradictions. Pain and struggle are inseparable from it, as in Adorno's own effort to wrest Hegel's truth from his untruth. Adorno's rejection of the notion of paying homage to the great man notwithstanding, his ultimate tribute to Hegel is the notion that he endured these efforts: "No philosophy was so profoundly rich; none held so unswervingly to the experience to which it had entrusted itself without reservation. Even the marks of its failure were struck by truth itself" ("Aspects"). And if the ultimate criticism of Hegel is that he is the bourgeois philosopher par excellence, the "comfortable professor lecturing unconcernedly on the sufferings of mankind," then the effacement of self that gives him this bourgeois plainness—the *Nüchternheit* that Walter Benjamin created his *Deutsche Menschen* to honor—is the self-divestiture that makes philosophical experience possible. As Adorno says, it is this sober dryness "to which the most extreme pathos shrivels in Hegel" that gives thought its dignity, just as, in a different tonality, it gives Adorno's appreciation its poignancy.

And is not Adorno himself, who was repeatedly accused of bourgeois elitism but whose countenance remained clear and whose speech was "druckfertig"—"print-ready"—speaking on his own behalf here as well, expressing the effacement of self and the surrender to mortality that informed his own attempt to immerse the self without reservation in its object? And is this dialectic of self-effacement and the ravaging travail of spirit in the individual not itself the new conception of the dialectic toward which *Hegel: Three Studies* labors, a conception whose energies will, we hope, in an age in which the individual is increasingly endangered, continue to sound across historical chasms?

The translator would like to thank Jeremy Shapiro, Quentin Smith, and Andrew Buchwalter for advice on difficult points in the text, Tom McCarthy and Larry Cohen for their unflagging support of the project, and Arden H. Nicholsen for a careful and appreciative reading of the manuscript in progress. Jan Miller of the Antioch College library staff deserves special thanks for literally going the extra mile to procure texts. As in her other translations of Adorno's work, the translator has attempted to preserve as many of the features of Adorno's prose as are consistent with intelligibility in English. For any resulting awkwardnesses (Adorno's word was "inconcinnities") she alone is responsible.

Preface

When it came time for a new edition of *Aspects of Hegel's Philosophy*, I wanted to supplement that text with the monograph on the experiential content of Hegel's philosophy that I had published in the meantime. What impelled me to go beyond this was the analogy with the saying *tres homines faciunt collegium:* three monographs make a book, even if it is a short one. Hence, in accordance with a long-cherished plan, I set down my thoughts on questions of understanding Hegel. They spring from my work in the Philosophisches Seminar at the University of Frankfurt. Over many years Max Horkheimer and I have often been concerned with Hegel there; my intention was to use what I had observed in the teaching situation as a point of departure. Given the unity of the philosophical thought of the two of us responsible for the relevant interpretations, it was possible to forgo individual references.

To avert disappointment, let me emphasize that "Skoteinos" does not claim to accomplish of itself the illumination of Hegel's main works, something that is long overdue. It merely formulates considerations of principle bearing on this task; at best it hazards guesses about how one would arrive at an understanding, without dispensing anyone from the efforts involved in concretizing those considerations with regard to the texts. The issue is not to make the reading of Hegel easier but to prevent the extraordinary exertions that Hegel requires, now as then, from being wasted. Something that Hegel reminds epistemology about should be applied to instructions about how to read Hegel as well: the instructions can prove successful only in the course of carrying out individual interpretations. The limits that the author of a propaedeutic must set for himself would thereby be transgressed. The fact that I have stopped precisely where I ought to begin may excuse some of the obvious inadequacies that displease me.

The work as a whole is intended as preparation for a revised conception of the dialectic.

Theodor W. Adorno
Frankfurt, summer 1963

A Note on the Text

"Aspects of Hegel's Philosophy" grew out of a talk I gave at the Free University of Berlin on November 14, 1956, commemorating the 125th anniversary of Hegel's death. The preliminary work was too extensive to be adequately incorporated into that talk. I was forced to select one complex, albeit a central one, for the Berlin talk and to deal with other motifs in a lecture broadcast on Hessian radio. But since the elements had been conceived as a whole, I then brought them together, with important additions, in a monograph.

Similarly, "The Experiential Content of Hegel's Philosophy" is a greatly expanded version of a lecture I gave at the meetings of the German Hegel Society in Frankfurt on October 25, 1958; I delivered it again shortly afterwards in French at the Sorbonne. It was printed in the *Archiv für Philosophie* 1959, vol. 9:1–2.

"Skoteinos," written in the winter of 1962–63, is unpublished.

Since the three complementary parts of the book had been given fixed literary form somewhat independently of one another, certain motifs are repeated, always, of course, from different perspectives.

I would like to express my heartfelt gratitude to the assistants at the Philosophisches Seminar at the University of Frankfurt, especially Professor Hermann Schweppenhäuser, Dr. Alfred Schmidt, Dr. Werner Becker, and Dr. Herbert Schnädelbach.

Theodor W. Adorno

Editorial Remarks from the German Edition

The notes Adorno himself provided on the genesis of *Hegel: Three Studies* require few additions.

The first of the three studies was published separately by Suhrkamp Verlag, Berlin and Frankfurt am Main, in 1957, under the title *Aspects of Hegel's Philosophy.* That edition contains a motto taken from Adorno's *Minima Moralia:* "Das Ganze ist das Unwahre" [the whole is the untrue]. A "note" to that edition dated January 1957 was incorporated into the "Note" in *Hegel: Three Studies,* with the exception of the last paragraph, which reads: "A publication about Hegel offers an opportunity to repeat that the philosophical thought of the author and that of Max Horkheimer are one and the same. For this reason it has been possible to forgo individual references."

The three studies were put together as *Drei Studien zu Hegel* for the series "edition suhrkamp," and the first edition was published in 1963.

The text of *Hegel: Three Studies* is based on the third edition of 1969, the last to appear during the author's lifetime. A few corrections have been made on the basis of indications in the author's copy. The citations have been checked and corrections made where necessary. Four textual notes in "Skoteinos" have been moved from the endnotes to the pages to which they refer. Otherwise the form of the notes follows that of the original as far as possible; even the points in which they are inconsistent are an expression of Adorno's antipathy to unified systematic thought.

January 1971

Hegel

Three Studies

Aspects of Hegel's Philosophy

A historical occasion like the 125th anniversary of Hegel's death could have elicited what we call an "appreciation." But that concept has become untenable, if indeed it ever had any value. It makes the impudent claim that because one has the dubious good fortune to live later, and because one has a professional interest in the person one is to talk about, one can sovereignly assign the dead person his place, thereby in some sense elevating oneself above him. This arrogance echoes in the loathsome question of what in Kant, and now Hegel as well, has any meaning for the present—and even the so-called Hegel renaissance began half a century ago with a book by Benedetto Croce that undertook to distinguish between what was living and what was dead in Hegel. The converse question is not even raised: what the present means in the face of Hegel; whether perhaps the reason one imagines one has attained since Hegel's absolute reason has not in fact long since regressed behind the latter and accommodated to what merely exists, when Hegelian reason tried to set the burden of existence in motion through the reason that obtains even in what exists. All appreciations are subject to the judgment passed in Hegel's preface to the *Phenomenology of Spirit* on those who are above something only because they are not in it. Appreciations fail from the start to capture the seriousness and cogency of Hegel's philosophy by practicing on him what he called, with appropriate disdain, a philosophy of perspectives. If one does not want to miss Hegel with one's very first words, one must confront, however inadequately, the claim his philosophy makes to truth, rather than merely discussing his philosophy from above, and thereby from below.

Like other closed systems of thought, Hegel's philosophy avails itself of the dubious advantage of not having to allow any criticism whatsoever. All criticism of the details, according to Hegel, remains partial and misses the whole, which in any case takes this criticism into account. Conversely, criticizing the whole as a whole is abstract, "unmediated," and ignores the fundamental motif of Hegelian philosophy: that it cannot be distilled into any "maxim" or general principle and proves its worth only as a totality, in the concrete interconnections of all its moments. Accordingly, the only way to honor Hegel is to refuse to allow oneself to be intimidated by the virtually mythological complexity of his critical method, which makes criticism seem false no matter what, and instead of graciously or ungraciously listing or denying his merits, go after the whole, which is what Hegel himself was after.

These days it is hardly possible for a theoretical idea of any scope to do justice to the experience of consciousness, and in fact not only the experience of consciousness but the embodied experience of human beings, without having incorporated something of Hegel's philosophy. But this cannot be explained in terms of the trivial aperçu according to which Hegel, the absolute idealist, was a great realist and a man with a sharp historical eye. Hegel's substantive insights, which extended to the irreconcilability of the contradictions in bourgeois society, cannot be separated from speculation—the vulgar notion of which has nothing to do with the Hegelian notion—as though it were some kind of troublesome ornamentation. On the contrary, those insights are produced by speculation, and they lose their substance as soon as they are conceived as merely empirical. The idea that the a priori is also the a posteriori, an idea that was programmatic in Fichte and was then fully elaborated by Hegel, is not an audacious piece of bombast; it is the mainspring of Hegel's thought: it inspires both his criticism of a grim empirical reality and his critique of a static apriorism. Where Hegel compels his material to speak, the idea of an original identity of subject and object "in spirit," an identity that becomes divided and then reunites, is at work. Otherwise the inexhaustibly rich content of his system would remain either a mere accumulation of facts, and thus prephilosophical, or merely dogmatic and without rigor. Richard Kroner rightly opposed describing the history of German Idealism as advancing directly from Schelling to Hegel. Rather, Hegel resisted the dogmatic moment in Schelling's philosophy of nature through recourse to a Fichtean, and even Kantian, epistemological impulse. The dynamic of the *Phenomenology of Spirit* begins in epistemology and then goes on, of course, as the introduction already indicates, to explode the position of an isolated or, in Hegelian terms, abstract epistemology. Accordingly, the abundance of experiential concreteness [*das Gegenständliche*] that is interpreted by thought in Hegel and nourishes thought in turn, is due not so much to a realistic frame of mind on Hegel's part as to his method of anamnesis, spirit's immersion in itself, or, in Hegel's words, being's inwardization and self-possession [*das in sich Hineingehen, sich Zusammenziehen des Seins*]. If one tried to rescue the material substance of Hegelian philosophy from its allegedly outmoded and arbitrary speculation by eradicating its idealism, one would have nothing but positivism on the one hand and superficial intellectual history on the other. What Hegel thought, however, is also of a completely different order than that of embeddedness in relationships to which the individual disciplines closed their eyes. His sytem is not an overarching scientific system any more than it is an agglomeration of witty observations. When one studies his work, it sometimes seems as though the progress that spirit imagines itself to have made, through clear methodology and iron-clad empiricism, since Hegel's death and in opposition to him, is all a regression, while the philosophers who think they are maintaining something of Hegel's legacy have for the most part missed the concrete content on which Hegel's thought first proved itself.

Think, for instance, of Gestalt theory, which Köhler expanded to a kind of philosophy. Hegel recognized the primacy of the whole over its finite parts, which are inadequate and, in their confrontation with the whole, contradictory. But he neither derived a metaphysics from the abstract principle of totality nor glorified the whole as such in the name of the "good Gestalt." He does not make the parts, as elements of the whole, autonomous in opposition to it; at the same time, as a critic of romanticism, he knows that the whole realizes itself only in and through the parts, only through discontinuity, alienation, and reflection—through, in short, everything that is anathema to Gestalt theory. If Hegel's whole exists at all it is only as the quintessence of the partial moments, which always point beyond themselves and are generated from one another; it does not exist as something beyond them. This is what his category of totality is intended to convey. It is incompatible with any kind of tendency to harmony, no matter how much the late Hegel may subjectively have had such tendencies. His critical thought goes beyond both the stating of the unconnected and the principle of continuity; in him, connection is not a matter of unbroken transition but a matter of sudden change, and the process takes place not through the moments approaching one another but through rupture. Modern Gestalt theory as interpreted by Max Scheler challenges traditional epistemological subjectivism and interprets the chaotic material of the senses, the givenness of the phenomenon, which the whole Kantian tradition had disqualified, as already specified and structured. Hegel, however, emphasized precisely this specification of the object, without in the process idolizing the sense certainty with the critique of which the *Phenomenology of Spirit* begins, to say nothing of intellectual intuition. It is precisely through absolute idealism, which permits nothing to remain outside the subject, now expanded to become infinite, but instead sweeps everything along with it into the current of immanence, that the opposition between mere matter and a consciousness that bestows form and meaning is extinguished. All later criticism of the so-called formalism of epistemology and ethics can be found explicitly formulated in Hegel, but he did not therefore leap with a bound into the allegedly concrete as did Schelling before him and existential ontology today. One consequence of the unrestrained expansion of the subject to absolute spirit in Hegel is that, as moments inherent in this spirit, not only the subject but also the object are presented as substantial and making the full demands of their own beings. Hegel's much-admired material richness is itself a function of his speculative thought. It was his speculative thought that helped him to say something essential not merely about the instruments of knowledge but about its essential objects, without ever suspending consciousness's critical self-reflection. To the extent to which one can speak of realism in Hegel, it is to be found in the path followed by his idealism; it is not something heterogeneous to it. In Hegel the tendency of idealism is to move beyond itself.

Even the point of most extreme idealism in Hegel's thought, the subject-object construction, should by no means be dismissed as the arrogance of the unrestrained concept. In Kant, the idea that a world divided into subject and object, the world in which, as prisoners of our own constitution, we are involved only with phenomena, is not the ultimate world, already forms the secret source of energy. Hegel adds an un-Kantian element to that: the idea that in grasping, conceptually, the block, the limit that is set to subjectivity, in understanding subjectivity as "mere" subjectivity, we have already passed beyond that limit. Hegel, who in many respects is a Kant come into his own, is driven by the idea that knowledge, if there is such a thing, is by its very idea total knowledge, that every one-sided judgment intends, by its very form, the absolute, and does not rest until it has been sublated in it. Speculative idealism does not recklessly disregard the limits of the possibility of knowledge; rather, it searches for words to express the idea that a reference to truth as such is in fact inherent in all knowledge that is knowledge; that if it is to be knowledge at all and not a mere duplication of the subject, knowledge is more than merely subjective; it is objectivity like the objective reason in Plato, the legacy of which chemically permeates subjective transcendental philosophy in Hegel. In proper Hegelian terms one might say—at the same time altering him in crucial respects through interpretation that subjects him to a further round of reflection—that it is precisely the construction of the absolute subject in Hegel that does justice to an objectivity indissoluble in subjectivity. Paradoxically, historically, only absolute idealism gives free rein to the method that the introduction to the *Phenomenology of Spirit* calls "simply looking on" [*reines Zusehen*]. Hegel is able to think from the thing itself out, to surrender passively, as it were, to its authentic substance, only because by virtue of the system the matter at hand is referred to its identity with absolute subject. Things themselves speak in a philosophy that focuses its energies on proving that it is itself one with them.

No matter how much Hegel the Fichtean emphasizes the idea of "positing," of generation through spirit, no matter how thoroughly active and practical his concept of development is, he is at the same time passive in his respect for the specific, comprehending which means nothing other than obeying its own concept. The notion of spontaneous receptivity plays a role in Husserl's phenomenology. This idea too is Hegelian through and through, except that in Hegel it is not limited to a specific type of act of consciousness; it develops at all levels of both subjectivity and objectivity. Hegel everywhere yields to the object's own nature, which everywhere becomes something immediate for him again, but it is precisely this kind of subordination to the discipline of the thing itself that requires the most intense efforts on the part of the concept. Those efforts succeed at the moment in which the intentions of the subject are extinguished in the object. Hegel's critique strikes at the empty center of the static analysis of knowledge into subject and object that the currently accepted logic of science takes for granted, the residual theory of truth according to which the objective is what is left after the so-called subjective factors have been eliminated, and the blow he strikes is so deadly because he does not set up an irrational unity of subject and object in opposition to that analysis but instead preserves the distinct moments of the subjective and the objective while grasping them as mediated by one another. The insight that in the realm of the so-called *Geisteswissenschaften* [human sciences; literally, sciences of the spirit], wherever the object itself is mediated by "spirit," knowledge becomes fruitful not by excluding the subject but through its utmost exertions, through all its impulses and experiences—this insight, which self-reflection is now forcing upon the resistant social sciences, comes from Hegel's system. That insight makes his system scientifically superior to the institution of science and scholarship, which, while raging against the subject, regresses to a prescientific recording of mere unrelated facts, events, and opinions, a recording of what is most inadequately and contingently subjective. Although Hegel surrenders without reservation to the specificity of his object—actually to the objective dynamic of society—he is thoroughly immune, by virtue of his conception of the relationship between subject and object, which extends into all substantive knowledge, to the temptation to accept the facade uncritically: there are good reasons why the dialectic of essence and appearance is moved to the center of the *Logic*. This needs to be remembered at a time when those who administer the dialectic in its materialist version, the official thought of the East bloc, have debased it to an unreflected copy theory. Once divested of its critical ferment, the dialectic is as well suited to dogmatism as the immediacy of Schelling's intellectual intuition, against which Hegel's polemic was directed. Hegel helped Kant's critical philosophy come into its own by criticizing the Kantian dualism of form and content, by drawing the rigid determinations of difference of Kant—and, in Hegel's interpretation, Fichte as well—into a dynamic without sacrificing the indissolubility of the moments to a flat, unmediated identity. For Hegel's idealism, reason becomes a critical reason in a sense that criticizes Kant once again, a negative reason that both preserves static elements and sets them in motion. The poles that Kant opposed to one another—form and content, nature and spirit, theory and praxis, freedom and necessity, the thing in itself and the phenomenon—are all permeated through and through by reflection in such a way that none of these determinations are left standing as ultimate. In order to be thought, and to exist, each inherently requires the other that Kant opposed to it. Hence for Hegel mediation is never a middle element between extremes, as, since Kierkegaard, a deadly misunderstanding has depicted it as being;

instead, mediation takes place in and through the extremes, in the extremes themselves. This is the radical aspect of Hegel, which is incompatible with any advocacy of moderation. Hegel shows that the fundamental ontological contents that traditional philosophy hoped to distill are not ideas discretely set off from one another; rather, each of them requires its opposite, and the relationship of all of them to one another is one of process. But this alters the meaning of ontology so decisively that it seems futile to apply the word, as many contemporary interpreters of Hegel would like to do, to a so-called fundamental structure whose very nature is not to be a fundamental structure, not to be ὑποχείμενον, or substratum. In Kant's sense no world, no *constitutum,* is possible without the subjective conditions of reason, the *constituens,* and Hegel's self-reflection of idealism, similarly, adds that there can be no *constituens* and no generative conditions of the spirit that are not abstracted from actual subjects and thereby ultimately from something that is not merely subjective, from the "world." By virtue of this insistent response, the deadly legacy of traditional metaphysics, the question of an ultimate principle from which everything must be derivable, became meaningless for Hegel.

Hence the dialectic, the epitome of Hegel's philosophy, cannot be likened to a methodological or ontological principle that would characterize his philosophy the way the doctrine of ideas characterizes Plato in his middle period or the monadology characterizes Leibniz. The dialectic is neither a mere method by which spirit might elude the cogency of its object—in Hegel the dialectic literally accomplishes the opposite, the permanent confrontation of the object with its concept—nor is it a weltanschauung into whose schema one has to squeeze reality. Just as the dialectic does not favor individual definitions, so there is no definition that fits it. Dialectic is the unswerving effort to conjoin reason's critical consciousness of itself and the critical experience of objects. The scientific concept of verification makes its home in that realm of separate, rigid concepts, such as those of theory and experience, on which Hegel declared war. If, however, one were to make precise inquiries into its own verification, then it is precisely Hegel's conception of the dialectic, which the ignorant tend to dismiss as a conceptual straitjacket, that the most recent phase of history has verified. And it has done so to an extent that passes judgment on any attempt to orient oneself in terms of what simply is the case and to do without the alleged arbitrariness of the dialectical construction: in terms of his own ideology, and as the henchman of more powerful interests, Hitler attempted to eradicate bolshevism, whereas it was his war that brought the giant shadow of the Slavic world down on Europe—that same Slavic world of which Hegel had already made the ominous statement that it had not yet entered history. But it was not a prophetic historical gaze—something for which he would have had nothing but contempt—that enabled Hegel to say this; rather, it was the constructive force that enters fully into what is, without sacrificing itself as reason, critique, and the awareness of possibility.

For all that, however, and although the dialectic demonstrates the impossibility of reducing the world to a fixed subjective pole and methodically pursues the reciprocal negation and production of the subjective and objective moments, Hegel's philosophy, a philosophy of spirit, held fast to idealism. Only the doctrine of the identity of subject and object inherent in idealism—an identity that amounts in terms of form to the primacy of the subject—gives it the strength of totality that performs the negative labor—the dissolution of individual concepts, the reflection of the immediate and then the sublation of reflection. The most extreme formulations of this are to be found in Hegel's history of philosophy. Not only is Fichtean philosophy the completion of Kantian philosophy, as Fichte himself had repeatedly asserted, but, Hegel goes so far as to say, "In addition to these [that is, Kant's and Fichte's] systems of philosophies, and that of Schelling, there are none."[1] Like Fichte, Hegel attempted to outdo Kant in idealism by dissolving anything not proper to consciousness—in other words, the given moment of reality—into a positing by the infinite subject. Hegel praised the greater consistency of Kant's successors in comparison with the abysmal discontinuities of the Kantian system, and he even outdid them in this regard. It did not occur to him that the Kantian discontinuities register the very moment of nonidentity that is an indispensable part of his own conception of the philosophy of identity. Instead, he passes this judgment on Fichte: "The shortcoming in the Kantian philosophy was its unthinking inconsistency, through which speculative unity was lacking to the whole system; and this shortcoming was removed by Fichte. . . . Fichte's philosophy is thus the development of form in itself (reason is in itself a synthesis of concept and actuality), and in particular, a more consistent presentation of Kantian philosophy."[2] His agreement with Fichte extends still farther: "The Fichtian philosophy has the great advantage of having set forth the fact that Philosophy must be a science derived from one supreme principle, from which all determinations are necessarily derived. The important point is this unity of principle and the attempt to develop from it in a scientifically consistent way the whole content of consciousness, or, as has been said, to construct the whole world."[3] There is little that could demonstrate Hegel's self-contradictory relationship to idealism, whose highest peak and whose turning point he attained, more incisively than these sentences. For the content of Hegel's philosophy is the notion that truth—which in Hegel means the system—cannot be expressed as a fundamental principle of this kind, an ur-principle, but is the dynamic totality of all the propositions that can be generated from one another by virtue of their contradictions. But this is the exact opposite of Fichte's attempt to derive the world from pure identity, from absolute subject, from the one original positing. Despite this, however, Hegel considers the Fichtean postulate of the deductive system emphatically valid. It was only that he accorded its second principle much more weight than Fichte did in his *Science of Knowledge*. Matters do not rest with the "absolute form," to use Hegel's language, that Fichte took up and that is to enclose reality within it; instead, concrete reality itself is something constructed through the process whereby thought grasps the opposition of content to form and the opposing content, if you like, is developed out of the form itself. In his decision to tolerate no limits, to eliminate every particle of a determination of difference, Hegel literally oudid Fichtean idealism. The individual Fichtean principles thereby lose their conclusive significance. Hegel recognized the inadequacy of an abstract principle beyond the dialectic, a principle from which all else is to follow. Something that was implicit in Fichte but not yet developed now becomes the driving force of Hegel's philosophical activity. The consequence of the principle negates the principle itself and destroys its absolute primacy. Hence in the *Phenomenology* Hegel could start with the subject and grasp all concrete content in the contemplation of the subject's self-movement while on the other hand, in the *Logic*, he could have the movement of thought begin with being. Correctly understood, the choice of a starting point, of what comes first, is a matter of indifference in Hegel's philosophy; his philosophy does not recognize a first something of this kind as a fixed principle that remains inalterable and identical with itself as thought progresses. With this, Hegel leaves all traditional metaphysics, and the prespeculative notion of idealism as well, far behind. Nevertheless he does not abandon idealism. The absolute rigor and closed quality of the argument that he and Fichte strove for in opposition to Kant already establishes the priority of spirit, even if the subject is defined as object at every stage, just as conversely the object is defined as subject. When the contemplating spirit presumes to show that everything that exists is commensurable with spirit itself, with Logos and the determinations of thought, spirit sets itself up as an ontological ultimate, even if at the same time it grasps the untruth in this, that of the abstract a priori, and attempts to do away with its own fundamental thesis. In the objectivity of the Hegelian dialectic, which quashes all mere subjectivism, there is something like a will on the part of the subject to jump over its own shadow. The Hegelian subject-object is subject. This illuminates something that from the point of view of Hegel's own demand for complete consistency is an unresolved contradiction, the fact that the subject-object dialectic, which involves no abstract higher-level concept, itself constitutes the whole and yet is realized in turn as the life of absolute spirit. The quintessence of the conditioned, according to Hegel, is the unconditioned. It is this, not least of all, that gives rise to the hovering, suspended quality of Hegelian philosophy, its quality of being up in the air, its permanent *skandalon:* the name of the highest speculative concept, that of the absolute, of something utterly detached, is literally the name of that suspended quality. The Hegelian *skandalon* cannot be ascribed to any confusion or lack of clarity; rather, it is the price Hegel has to pay for absolute consistency, which comes up against the limits of consistent thought without being able to do away with them. Hegelian dialectic finds its ultimate truth, that of its own impossibility, in its unresolved and vulnerable quality, even if, as the theodicy of self-consciousness, it has no awareness of this.

With this, however, Hegel renders himself vulnerable to the critique of idealism: an immanent criticism, such as he required all criticism to be. He himself reached its threshold. Richard Kroner characterizes Hegel's relation to Fichte in words that in a certain sense already fit Fichte: "Insofar as the 'I' is opposed to all else through reflection, it is not distinguished from all else; to that extent it belongs instead to what it is opposed to, to what is posited, to the contents of thought, the moments of its activity."[4] German Idealism's response to this insight into the conditioned nature of the "I," another of the insights that the philosophy of reflection in its modern scientific form has only laboriously regained, is, roughly, the Fichtean distinction between the individual and the subject, in the last analysis the Kantian distinction between the "I" as the substratum of empirical psychology and the transcendental "I think." The finite subject is, as Husserl said of it, a part of the world. Itself tainted with relativity, it cannot be used to ground the absolute. It already presupposes—as the Kantian *constitutum,* that which is constituted—what transcendental philosophy is to explain. The "I think," in contrast, pure identity, is taken to be pure in the emphatic Kantian sense, independent of all spatiotemporal facticity. Only in this way can everything that exists dissolve without remainder in its concept. In Kant this step had not yet been taken. Just as on the one hand the categorial forms of the "I think" need a supplementary content that does not arise out of them themselves in order to make truth, that is, knowledge of nature, possible, so on the other hand the "I think" itself and the categorial forms are respected by Kant as a species of givens; to this extent at least the *Critique of Pure Reason* is more a phenomenology of subjectivity than a speculative system. In the "uns" [us] that Kant, in his introspective naiveté, continues to use unreflectively, he acknowledges the relationship—and not only in their application but in their origin—of the categorical forms to something existing, namely human beings, that arises in turn from the interplay of the forms with sensory material. Kant's reflections broke off at this point, thereby bearing witness to the irreducibility of the empirical to spirit, the interweaving of the moments. Fichte was not content with this. He relentlessly drove the distinction between the transcendental and the empirical subject beyond Kant, and because of the irreconcilability of the two he tried to extricate the principle of the "I" from facticity and thereby justify idealism in the absoluteness that then became the medium of the Hegelian system. Fichte's radicalism thereby revealed something that in Kant was hidden in the twilight of transcendental phenomenology, but Fichte also thereby involuntarily revealed the dubious nature of his own absolute subject. He calls it something that all later idealists, and certainly the ontologists among them, were most careful to avoid calling it: an abstraction.[5] Nevertheless, the pure "I" is to determine what it is abstracted from and what it itself is determined by, in that its very concept cannot be thought without such abstraction. What results from abstraction can never be made absolutely autonomous vis à vis what it is abstracted from; because the *abstractum* remains applicable to that which is subsumed within it, and because return is to be possible, the quality of what it has been abstracted from is always, in a certain sense, preserved in it at the same time, even if in an extremely general form. Hence if the formation of the concept of the transcendental subject or the absolute spirit sets itself completely outside individual consciousness as something spatiotemporal, when in fact the concept is achieved through individual consciousness, then the concept itself can no longer be made good; otherwise that concept, which did away with all fetishes, becomes a fetish itself, and speculative philosophy since Fichte has failed to see that. Fichte hypostatized the "I" that had been abstracted, and in this respect Hegel adhered to what he did. Both Fichte and Hegel skipped over the fact that the expression "I," whether it is the pure transcendental "I" or the empirical, unmediated "I," must necessarily designate some consciousness or other. Giving an anthropological-materialist turn to this polemic, Schopenhauer had already insisted on that in his critique of Kant. At least in moral philosophy, he says, Kant's pure reason is

taken . . . not as an intellectual faculty of man, though it is indeed nothing but this; on the contrary, it is hypostasized as something existing by itself, without any authority; and the deplorable philosophy of our times can serve as an illustration of the results of that most pernicious example and precedent. However, this laying down of morals not for men as men, but for all rational beings as such, is something so near to his heart, such a favorite notion of his, that Kant is never tired of repeating it on every occasion. I say, on the contrary, that we are never entitled to set up a genus that is given to us only in a single species, for into the concept of that genus we could bring absolutely nothing but what we had taken from this one species, and thus what we stated about the genus could always be understood only of the one species. On the other hand, by thinking away without authority what belongs to this species in order to form the genus, we should perhaps remove the very condition of the possibility of the remaining attributes that are hypostasized as genus.[6]

But even in Hegel the most emphatic expressions, such as spirit and self-consciousness, are derived from the finite subject's experience of itself and trudly do not stem from linguistic sloppiness; Hegel too is unable to cut the tie binding absolute spirit to the empirical person. No matter how thoroughly the Fichtean or Hegelian absolute "I," as an abstraction from the empirical "I," may erase the latter's specific contents, if it were no longer at all what it was abstracted from, namely "I," if it completely divested itself of the facticity contained in its concept, it would no longer be that being-with-itself of spirit, that homeland of knowledge from which the primacy of subjectivity in the great idealist systems depends. An "I" that was no longer "I" in any sense at all, an "I," that is, without any relation to individuated consciousness and thereby to the spatiotemporal person, would be nonsense. It would not only be as free-floating and indeterminable as Hegel accused being, its counterconcept, of being; in addition, it could no longer be grasped as an "I," as something mediated by consciousness. Analysis of the absolute subject has to acknowledge the indissolubility of an empirical, nonidentical moment in it, a moment that doctrines of the absolute subject, idealist systems of identity, are not permitted to acknowledge as indissoluble. In this sense Hegel's philosophy is untrue when measured against its own concept. In what sense is it then nevertheless true?

To answer this question one must elucidate something that dominates the whole of Hegel's philosophy without ever being made tangible. That is spirit. Spirit is not placed in absolute contrast to something nonspiritual, something material; originally it is not a sphere of particular objects, those of the later *Geisteswissenschaften.* Rather, it is unqualified and absolute: hence in Hegel, as a legacy of Kant's practical reason, it is explicitly called free. According to the definition in the *Encyclopedia,* however, it is "essentially active, productive,"[7] just as Kant's practical reason is essentially distinguished from theoretical reason in creating its "object," the deed. The Kantian moment of spontaneity, which is virtually equated with constitutive identity in the synthetic unity of apperception—Kant's concept of the "I think" was the formula for the lack of distinction between productive spontaneity and logical identity—becomes total in Hegel, and in this totality it becomes a principle of being no less than a principle of thought. But when Hegel no longer opposes production and deed to matter as subjective accomplishments but rather looks for them in specific objects, in concrete material reality, he comes close to the mystery behind synthetic apperception and takes it out of the mere arbitrary hypostasis of the abstract concept. The mystery, however, is none other than social labor. In the economic and philosophical manuscripts of the young Marx, discovered in 1932, this was recognized for the first time: "The outstanding achievement of Hegel's *Phenomenology*—the dialectic of negativity as the moving and creating principle—is . . . that he . . . grasps the nature of labour, and conceives objective man (true, because real man) as the result of his own labour."[8] The moment of universality in the active, transcendental subject as opposed to the merely empirical, isolated, and contingent subject, is no more a fantasy than is the validity of logical propositions as opposed to the empirical course of individual acts of thought. Rather, this universality is an expression of the social nature of labor, an expression both precise and concealed from itself for the sake of the general idealist thesis; labor only becomes labor as something for something else, something commensurable with other things, something that transcends the contingency of the individual subject. Aristotle's *Politics* already tells us that the self-preservation of individual subjects depends as much on the labor of others as society depends on the deeds of individuals. The reference of the productive moment of spirit back to a universal subject rather than to an individual who labors is what defines labor as something organized, something social; its own "rationality," the ordering of functions, is a social relationship.

Translating Hegel's concept of spirit into social labor elicits the reproach of a sociologism that confuses the genesis and influence of Hegel's philosophy with its substance. There is no question that Hegel was a transcendental analytic philosopher like Kant. One could show in detail how Hegel, as Kant's critic, sought to do justice to Kant's intentions by going beyond the

Critique of Pure Reason, just as Fichte's *Science of Knowledge* had pushed the limits of Kant's concept of the pure. The Hegelian categories, and especially the category of spirit, fall within the domain of transcendental constituents. But in Hegel, society, as the functional complex of empirical persons, would be what Kant calls a *constitutum,* a part of the existence that in Hegel's *Logic*— in Hegel's doctrine of the absolutely unconditioned and of existence as something that has come into being[9]—is in turn developed out of the absolute that Hegel says is spirit. The interpretation of spirit as society, accordingly, appears to be a μετάβασις εἰς ἄλλο γένος, a shift to something of a different kind incompatible with the sense of Hegel's philosophy if only because it does not satisfy the precept of immanent criticism and attempts to grasp the truth content of Hegelian philosophy in terms of something external to it, something that his philosophy, within its own framework, would have derived as conditioned or posited. Explicit critique of Hegel, of course, could show that he was not successful in that deduction. The linguistic expression "existence," which is necessarily conceptual, is confused with what it designates, which is nonconceptual, something that cannot be melted down into identity.[10] Immanently, Hegel cannot maintain the absoluteness of spirit, and his philosophy attests to that itself, at least insofar as it never finds the absolute except in the totality of disunity, in unity with its other. Conversely, however, society for its part is not mere existence, not mere fact. Only for a thought that works through external antitheses, a thought that is abstract in Hegel's sense, would the relationship of spirit and society be a transcendental-logical relationship between *constituens* and *constitutum.* Society is allotted precisely what Hegel reserves for spirit as opposed to all the isolated individual moments of empirical reality. Those moments are mediated by society, constituted the way things are constituted by spirit for an idealist, prior to any particular influence exerted by society on phenomena: society is manifested in phenomena the way, for Hegel, essence is manifested in them. Society is essentially concept, just as spirit is. As the unity of human subjects who reproduce the life of the species through their labor, things come into being within society objectively, independent of reflection, without regard to the specific qualities of those who labor or the products of labor. The principle of the equivalence of social labor makes society in its modern bourgeois sense both something abstract and the most real thing of all, just what Hegel says of the emphatic notion of the concept. Hence every step thought takes comes up against society, and no step can pin it down as such, as one thing among other things. What permits Hegel the dialectician to preserve the concept of spirit from contamination with brute fact, and thereby to sublimate the brutality of the factual into spirit and legitimate it, is itself secondary. For the subject reflecting on it, the experience, itself unconscious, of abstract labor takes on magical form. For that subject, labor becomes its own reflected form, a pure deed of spirit, spirit's productive unity. For nothing is to be external to spirit. But the brute fact that disappears in the totalized notion of spirit returns in that notion as a logical compulsion. The individual fact can no more avoid it than the individual person can avoid the *contrainte sociale*. It is only this brutality of coercion that creates the semblance of reconciliation in the doctrine of an identity that has been produced.

Even before Hegel, the expressions through which spirit was defined as original production in idealist systems were all without exception derived from the sphere of labor. No other expressions could be found, because in terms of its own meaning, what the transcendental synthesis was after could not be separated from its connection with labor. The systematically regulated activity of reason turns labor inward; the burdensomeness and coerciveness of outwardly directed labor has perpetuated itself in the reflective, modeling efforts that knowledge directs toward its "object," efforts that are again required for the progressive domination of nature. Even the traditional distinction between sensibility and understanding, *Sinnlichkeit* and *Verstand,* indicates that in contrast to what is merely given by sensibility, without compensation, as it were, the understanding does something: what is given through the senses is simply there, like the fruits of the field, but the operations of the understanding are subject to volition. As that through which human beings form something that then confronts them, those operations can occur or not occur. The primacy of Logos has always been part of the work ethic. The stance adopted by thought as such, regardless of its content, is a confrontation with nature that has become habitual and has been internalized; an intervention and not a mere reception. Hence talk about thought is always accompanied by talk about a material that thought knows to be distinct from itself, a material it processes the way labor processes its raw materials. For thought is always accompanied by the moment of violent exertion—a reflection of the dire necessities of life—that characterizes labor; the strains and toils of the concept are not metaphorical.

The Hegel of the *Phenomenology,* in whom the consciousness of spirit as living activity and its identity with the real social subject was less atrophied than in the later Hegel, recognized the spontaneous spirit as labor, if not in theory at least in his language. The path natural consciousness follows to the identity of absolute knowledge [*Wissen*] is itself labor. The relationship of spirit to what is given manifests itself on the model of a social process, a process of labor: "Knowledge in its first phase, or immediate Spirit, is the non-spiritual, i.e. sense-consciousness. In order to become genuine knowledge, to beget the element of

Science which is the pure Notion of Science itself, it must travel a long way and work its passage."[11] This is by no means a figure of speech: if spirit is to be real, then its labor is certainly real. The Hegelian "labor of the concept" is not a loose circumlocution for the activity of the scholar. Hegel always represents the latter, as philosophy, as passive, "looking on," as well, and for good reasons. The philosopher's labor actually aims solely at helping to express what is active in the material itself, what, as social labor, has an objective form that confronts human beings and yet remains the labor of human beings. "The movement in which the unessential consciousness strives to attain this oneness," Hegels says in a later passage in the *Phenomenology*, "is itself threefold in accordance with the threshold relation this consciousness will have with its incarnate beyond: first, as pure consciousness; second, as a particular individual who approaches the actual world in the form of desire and work; and third, as consciousness that is aware of its own being-for-itself."[12]

Interpreters of Hegel have rightly insisted that each of the primary moments distinguished within his philosophy is at the same time the whole as well. But that is certainly also true of the concept of labor as a relationship to reality: for the dialectic as such, as a dialectic of the subject-object identity, is precisely such a relationship. The crucial connection between the concepts of desire and labor removes the latter from the position of a mere analogy to the abstract activity of abstract spirit. Labor in the full sense is in fact tied to desire, which it in turn negates: it satisfies the needs of human beings on all levels, helps them in their difficulties, reproduces human life, and demands sacrifices of them in return. Even in its intellectual form, labor provides a longer arm with which to procure the means of life; it is the principle of the domination of nature, which has become autonomous and thereby alienated from its knowledge of itself. But idealism becomes false when it mistakenly turns the totality of labor into something existing in itself, when it sublimates its principle into a metaphysical one, into the *actus purus* of spirit, and tendentially transfigures something produced by human beings, something fallible and conditioned, along with labor itself, which is the suffering of human beings, into something eternal and right. If one were permitted to speculate about Hegel's speculation, one might surmise that the extension of spirit to become totality is the inversion of the recognition that spirit is precisely not an isolated principle, not some self-sufficient substance, but rather a moment of social labor, the moment that is separate from physical labor. But physical labor is necessarily dependent on something other than itself, on nature. Labor—and in the last analysis its reflective form, spirit, as well—cannot be conceived without the concept of nature, any more than can nature without labor: the two are distinct from and mediated by one another at the same time. Marx's *Critique of the Gotha Program* describes a state of affairs hidden deep within Hegel's philosophy, and does so all the more precisely in that it was not intended as a polemic against Hegel. Marx is discussing the familiar saying "labor is the source of all wealth and all culture," to which he counters,

Labor is not the source of all wealth. Nature is just as much the source of use values (and it is surely of such that material wealth consists!) as labor, which itself is only the manifestation of a force of nature, human labor power. The above phrase is to be found in all children's primers and is correct in so far as it is implied that labor is performed with the appurtenant subjects and instruments. But a socialist program cannot allow such bourgeois phrases to pass over in silence the conditions that alone give them meaning. And in so far as man from the beginning behaves towards nature, the primary source of all instruments and subjects of labor, as an owner, treats her as belonging to him, his labor becomes the source of use values, therefore also of wealth. The bourgeois have very good grounds for falsely ascribing supernatural creative power to labor; since precisely from the fact that labor depends on nature it follows that the man who possesses no other property than his labor power must, in all conditions of society and culture, be the slave of other men who have made themselves the owners of the material conditions of labor.[13]

But because of this Hegel cannot afford to express the separation of mental and manual labor, and he does not read spirit as an isolated aspect of labor but instead, conversely, dissolves labor into a moment of spirit; one might say he takes the rhetorical figure *pars pro toto* as his maxim. Detached from what is not identical with it, labor becomes ideology. Those who have at their disposal the labor of others ascribe to it inherent value, consider it absolute and primary, precisely because labor is only labor for others. The metaphysics of labor and the appropriation of the labor of others are complementary. This social relationship dictates the untruth in Hegel, the masking of the subject as subject-object, the denial of the nonidentical in the totality, no matter how much the nonidentical receives its due in the reflection of any particular judgment.

Apart from the chapter on lordship and bondage, in the *Phenomenology of Spirit* the nature of Hegel's productive spirit as labor appears, surprisingly, most graphically in the material on "natural religion," at the third stage of which the spiritual becomes religious content for the first time, as a "product of human labor":[14] "Spirit, therefore, here appears as an artificer, and its action whereby it produces itself as object but without having yet grasped the thought of itself is an instinctive operation, like the building of a honeycomb by bees. . . . The crystals of pyramids and obelisks . . . are the works of this artificer of rigid form."[15] In not simply opposing fetish worship to religion as a primitive or degenerate stage but instead defining it as a necessary moment in the formation of the religious spirit and thereby, in the sense of the *Phenomenology*'s subject-object dialectic, as a necessary moment in the formation of religion itself and ultimately of the absolute, Hegel includes human labor in its concrete material form among the essential characteristics of spirit as the absolute. Only a little more would be needed—remembrance of the simultaneously mediated and irrevocably natural moment in labor—and the Hegelian dialectic would reveal its identity and speak its own name.

With the separation of mental and manual labor, privilege reserves mental labor, which despite all assertions to the contrary is the easier, for itself. But at the same time manual labor always reappears in warning in the spiritual process, which is an imitation of physical action mediated by the imagination; spirit can never get completely free of its relationship to the nature it is to dominate. Spirit obeys nature in order to master it; even its proud sovereignty is purchased with suffering.[16] The metaphysics of spirit, however, which makes spirit, as labor unconscious of itself, an absolute, is the affirmation of its entanglement, an attempt on the part of a self-reflective spirit to reinterpret the curse to which it submits as a blessing by passing it on, and thereby to justify it. In this regard, especially, Hegel's philosophy can be accused of being ideological: in its exposition, taken to the extreme, of the bourgeois celebration of labor. It is precisely in this most elevated point of the idealist system, the absolute proclaimed ecstatically at the end of the *Phenomenology,* that the sober realistic features of Hegel take refuge. At the same time, even this deceptive identification of labor with the absolute had a valid basis. To the extent to which the world forms a system, it becomes one precisely through the closed universality of social labor; social labor is in fact radical mediation, both between man and nature and also within spirit, which exists for itself, which tolerates nothing outside itself and forbids remembrance of anything outside it. There is nothing in the world that shall not manifest itself to human beings solely through social labor. Even where labor has no power over it, pure nature is defined through its relationship to labor, even if that relationship is a negative one. Only awareness of all that could lead the Hegelian dialectic beyond itself, and it is precisely this awareness that is forbidden to it: it would pronounce the name that holds it in its spell. Because nothing is known but what has passed through labor, labor, rightly and wrongly, becomes something absolute, and disaster becomes salvation; this is why the whole, which is the part, compulsively and unavoidably occupies the position of truth in the science of manifesting consciousness. For the absolutization of labor is that of the class relationship: a humankind free of labor would be free of domination. Spirit knows that without being permitted to know it; this is the poverty of philosophy. But the step by which labor sets itself up as the metaphysical principle pure and simple is none other than the consistent elimination of the "material" to which all labor feels itself tied, the material that defines its boundary for it, reminds it of what is below it, and relativizes its sovereignty. This is why epistemology juggles things until the given gives the illusion of having been produced by spirit. The fact that spirit too stands under the compulsion of labor and is itself labor is to disappear; the great classical philosophy literally passes the quintessence of coercion off as freedom. It gets refuted because the reduction of what exists to spirit cannot succeed, because that epistemological position, as Hegel himself knew, must be abandoned in the course of its own development. But it has its truth, in that no one is capable of stepping out of the world constituted by labor into another and unmediated one. The identification of spirit with labor can be criticized only in confronting the philosophical concept of spirit with what that concept actually accomplishes and not through recourse to something transcendent, however positive its nature.

Spirit did not accomplish this. We know that in its emphatic Hegelian version, the concept of spirit is to be understood organically; the partial moments are to grow into and be interpenetrated by one another by virtue of a whole that is already inherent in every one of them. This concept of system implies the identity of subject and object, which has developed into the sole and conclusive absolute, and the truth of the system collapses when that identity collapses. But that identity, full reconciliation through spirit in a world which is in reality antagonistic, is a mere assertion. The philosophical anticipation of reconciliation is a trespass against real reconciliation; it ascribes anything that contradicts it to "foul" existence as unworthy of philosophy. But a seamless system and an achieved reconciliation are not one and the same; rather, they are contradictory: the unity of the system derives from unreconcilable violence. Satanically, the world as grasped by the Hegelian system has only now, a hundred and fifty years later, proved itself to be a system in the literal sense, namely that of a radically societalized society. One of the most remarkable aspects of Hegel's accomplishment is that he inferred that systematic character of society from the concept long before it could gain ascendancy in the sphere of Hegel's own experience, that of a Germany far behind in its bourgeois development. A world integrated through "production," through the exchange relationship, depends in all its moments on the social conditions of its production, and in that sense actually realizes the primacy of the whole over its parts; in this regard the desperate impotence of every single individual now verifies Hegel's extravagant conception of the system. Even the cult of production is more than the ideology of human beings who dominate nature and pursue their own interests without restraint. In that cult is sedimented the fact that the universal exchange relationship in which everything that exists, exists only for something else, stands under the domination of those who hold social production at their disposal; this domination is worshipped philosophically. Even the being-for-something-else that is the official justification for the existence of all commodities is only secondary to production. The very world in which nothing exists for its own sake is also the world of an unleashed production that forgets its human aims. The self-forgetfulness of production, the insatiable and destructive expansive principle of the exchange society, is reflected in Hegelian metaphysics. It describes the way the world actually is, not in historical perspective but in essence, without creating any blue smoke in the process with the question of authenticity.

Civil society is an antagonistic totality. It survives only in and through its antagonisms and is not able to resolve them. In the work by Hegel that is most notorious for its restorationist tendencies, its apology for the status quo, and its cult of the state, the *Philosophy of Right,* that is stated bluntly. The very eccentricities and provocative passages that are responsible for the fact that important thinkers in the West like Veblen, Dewey, and even Santayana have lumped Hegel together with German imperialism and fascism should themselves be seen as derived from Hegel's consciousness of the antagonistic character of the totality. This is why Hegel's idolization of the state should not be trivialized by being treated as a mere empirical aberration or an irrelevant addendum. Rather, that idolization is itself produced by insight into the fact that the contradictions of civil society cannot be resolved by its self-movement. Passages like this one are critical:

It hence becomes apparent that despite an excess of wealth civil society is not rich enough, i.e. its own resources are insufficient to check excessive poverty and the creation of a penurious rabble. . . . This inner dialectic of civil society thus drives it—or at any rate drives a specific civil society—to push beyond its own limits and seek markets, and so its necessary means of subsistence, in other lands which are either deficient in the goods it has over-produced, or else generally backward in industry, &c.[17]

The free play of forces in capitalist society, whose liberal economic economic theory Hegel had accepted, has no antidote for the fact that poverty, "pauperism" in Hegel's old-fashioned terminology, increases with social wealth; still less could Hegel envision an increase in production that would make a mockery of the assertion that society is not rich enough in goods. The state is appealed to in desperation as a seat of authority beyond this play of forces. Paragraph 249 expressly refers to the extremely advanced passage just quoted. The beginning of that paragraph reads,

While the public authority must also undertake the higher directive function of providing for the interests which lead beyond the borders of its society (see Paragraph 246), its primary purpose is to actualize and maintain the universal contained within the particularity of civil society, and its control takes the form of an external system and organization for the protection and security of particular ends and interests *en masse*, inasmuch as these interests subsist only in this universal.[18]

It is intended to allay something that could not otherwise be smoothed over. Hegel's philosophy of the state is a necessary tour de force; a tour de force because it suspends the dialectic under the aegis of a principle to which Hegel's own critique of the abstract could be applied, a principle whose locus, as Hegel at least suggests, is by no means outside the play of social forces:

Particular interests which are common to everyone fall within civil society and lie outside the absolutely universal interest of the state proper (see Paragraph 256). The administration of these is in the hands of Corporations (see Paragraph 251), commercial and professional as well as municipal, and their officials, directors, managers and the like. It is the business of the officials to manage the private property and interests of these particular spheres and, from that point of view, their authority rests on the confidence of their commonalties and professional equals. On the other hand, however, these circles of particular interests must be subordinated to the higher interests of the state, and hence the filling of positions of responsibility in Corporations, &c., will generally be effected by a mixture of popular election by those interested with appointment and ratification by higher authority.[19]

But the tour de force was necessary because otherwise the dialectical principle would have extended beyond what exists and thereby negated the thesis of absolute identity—and it is only absolute in that it is realized; that is the core of Hegel's philosophy. Nowhere does that philosophy come closer to the truth about its own substratum, society, that where it turns into nonsense when confronted with it. Hegel's philosophy is indeed essentially negative: critique. In extending the transcendental philosophy of the *Critique of Pure Reason* through the thesis of reason's identity with what exists and making it a critique of what exists, a critique of any and every positivity, Hegel denounced the world, whose theodicy constitutes his program, in its totality as well; he denounced it as a web of guilt [*Schuldzusammenhang*] in which, as Mephistopheles says in *Faust*, everything that exists deserves to perish. Even the false claim that the world is nonetheless a good world contains within it the legitimate demand that the empirical world become a good and a reconciled world, not merely in the Idea that is its opposite but in the flesh. If in the last analysis Hegel's system makes the transition into untruth by following its own logic, this is a judgment not simply on Hegel, as a self-righteous positivist science would like to think, but rather a judgment on reality. Hegel's scornful "so much the worse for the facts" is invoked against him so automatically only because it expresses the dead serious truth about the facts. Hegel did not simply reconstruct them in thought; he grasped them and criticized them by producing them in thought: their negativity always makes them into something other than what they merely are and claim to be. The principle of reality's becoming, through which it is more than its positivity, that is, the central idealist motor of Hegel's thought, is at the same time anti-idealist. It is the subject's critique of a reality that idealism equates with the absolute subject, namely consciousness of contradiction within the thing itself, and thereby the force of theory, a force with which the latter turns against itself. If Hegel's philosophy fails in terms of the highest criterion, its own, it thereby also proves itself true. The nonidentity of the antagonistic, a nonidentity it runs up against and laboriously pulls together, is the nonidentity of a whole that is not the true but the untrue, the absolute opposite of justice. But in reality this very nonidentity has the form of identity, an all-inclusiveness that is not governed by any third, reconciling element. This kind of deluded identity is the essence of ideology, of socially necessary illusion. Only through the process whereby the contradiction becomes absolute, and not through the contradiction becoming alleviated in the absolute, could it disintegrate and perhaps find its way to that reconciliation that must have misled Hegel because its real possibility was still concealed from him. In all its particular moments Hegel's philosophy is intended to be negative; but if, contrary to his intentions, it becomes negative as a whole as well, it thereby acknowledges the negativity of its object. In that ultimately the nonidentity of subject and object, concept and thing, idea and society, emerges, unpacifiable, in his philosophy; in that it ultimately disintegrates in absolute negativity, it nevertheless also redeems its promise and truly becomes identical with its ensnared subject matter. In the last analysis, even in Hegel the quiescence of movement, the absolute, means simply the reconciled life, the life of the pacified drive that no longer knows either deficiency or the labor to which alone, however, it owes that reconciliation. Hence the locus of Hegel's truth is not outside the system; rather, it is as inherent in the system as his untruth. For this untruth is none other than the untruth of the system of the society that constitutes the substratum of his philosophy.

The objective turn that idealism took in Hegel, the restitution of the speculative metaphysics that had been shattered by Kant's critical philosophy, a restitution that restores concepts like that of being and that wants to salvage even the ontological proof of God—all of this has encouraged people to claim Hegel for existential ontology. Heidegger's interpretation of the introduction to the *Phenomenology* in *Holzwege* is the most well known if by no means the first testimony to that. From this claim one can learn something that existential ontology is currently reluctant to hear—existential ontology's affinity with transcendental idealism, something it imagines it has overcome through the pathos of being. But while what now goes under the name of the question of being has a place as a moment in Hegel's system, Hegel denies being the very absoluteness, the very priority over all thought or concept, that the most recent resurrection of metaphysics hopes to secure. By virtue of its definition of being as an essentially negative, reflected, criticized moment of the dialectic, Hegel's theory of being becomes incompatible with the contemporary theologization of being. Scarcely anywhere does his philosophy have more contemporary relevance than where it dismantles the concept of being. Even the definition of being at the beginning of the *Phenomenology* says the precise opposite of what the word is intended to suggest today: "Further, the living Substance is being which is in truth Subject, or, what is the same, is in truth actual only in so far as it is the movement of positing itself, or is the mediation of its self-othering with itself."[20] The distinction between being as subject and the being [*Seyn*] written with the *y* that for Hegel was still orthographic but today is archaic, is the distinction that makes all the difference. In contrast to taking subjective consciousness as a point of departure, Hegel's *Logic*, as we know, develops the categories of thought itself from one another in their objectivity and in doing so begins with the concept of being. This beginning, however, does not found any *prima philosophia*. Hegel's being is the opposite of a primordial entity. Hegel does not credit the concept of being, as a primordial value, with immediacy, the illusion that being is logically and genetically prior to any reflection, any division between subject and object; instead, he eradicates immediacy. Being, he says at the beginning of the section of the *Logic* for which the word *being* serves as the title, is "indeterminate immediacy,"[21] and because of its indeterminateness, this very immediacy to which existential ontology clings becomes for Hegel, who understood the mediatedness of everything unmediated, an objection to the dignity of being; it is being's negativity, pure and simple, that motivates the dialectical step that equates being with nothingness: "In its indeterminate immediacy it is equal only to itself. . . . It is pure indeterminateness and emptiness. There is nothing to be intuited in it, if one can speak here of intuiting; or, it is only pure intuiting itself; just as little is anything to be thought in it, or it is equally only this empty thinking. Being, the indeterminate immediate, is in fact nothing, and neither more or less than nothing."[22] This emptiness, however, is not so much an ontological quality of being as a deficiency in the philosophical idea that terminates in being. "If we enunciate Being as a predicate of the absolute," writes Hegel at his most mature, in the *Encyclopedia,* "we get the first definition of the latter. The Absolute is Being. This is (in thought) the absolutely initial definition, the most abstract and stinted."[23] The concept of being, the ultimate legacy of Husserl's "originary intuition," is currently being celebrated as something removed from all reification, as absolute immediacy. Hegel not only saw that it is incapable of being grasped intuitively because of that indeterminateness and emptiness; he also saw that it is a concept that forgets it is a concept and masquerades as pure immediacy; in a certain sense it is the most thinglike concept of all. "When being is taken in this simplicity and immediacy, the recollection that it is the result of complete abstraction, and so for that reason alone is abstract negativity, nothing, is left behind . . . ,"[24] he writes at a somewhat later point in the *Logic.* But one can see from statements in the *Logic* directed specifically against Jacobi that Hegel is not engaging in sublime play with ur-words here; rather, the critique of being is in fact intended as a critique of any and every emphatic use of this concept in philosophy:

With this wholly abstract purity of continuity, that is, indeterminateness and vacuity of conception, it is indifferent whether this abstraction is called space, pure intuiting, or pure thinking; it is altogether the same as what the Indian calls Brahma, when for years on end, physically motionless and equally unmoved in sensation, conception, fantasy, desire, and so on, looking only at the tip of his nose, he says inwardly only Om, Om, Om, or else nothing at all. This dull, empty consciousness, understood as consciousness, is—being.[25]

Hegel heard the evocation of being in its manic rigidity as the formulaic clattering of the prayer wheel. He knew something that has currently been falsified and lost, for all the talk of the concrete; lost precisely in the magic of the undefined concreteness that has no substance but its own aura: that philosophy is not permitted to look for its subject matter in the most supreme universal concepts—which are then ashamed of their own universal conceptual character—for the sake of their presumed eternity and immutability. Like only the Nietzsche of the *Twilight of the Idols* after him, Hegel rejected the equation of philosophical substance—truth—with the highest abstractions, and located truth in the very specificities with which traditional metaphysics was too refined to dirty its hands. In Hegel idealism transcends itself not least of all in this intention, which he carries out magnificently in the close linking of stages of consciousness with sociohistorical stages in the *Phenomenology of Spirit*. What currently claims to rise above dialectics as an evocation of ur-words, as "*Sage*," now more than ever falls prey to the dialectic: it is abstraction, which inflates itself into a something that exists in and for itself and in so doing sinks down into something utterly without content, into tautology, into being that says nothing about being, over and over again.

Since Husserl, contemporary philosophies of being have revolted against idealism. To this extent the irrevocable situation of historical consciousness is expressed in them: they register the fact that what is cannot be developed or deduced from mere subjective immanence, from consciousness. But they thereby hypostatize the supreme result of subjective-conceptual abstraction, being, and thus, both in terms of their stance on society and in their theoretical approach, they are trapped within idealism without being aware of it. There is nothing that demonstrates this more strikingly than the speculations of the arch-idealist Hegel. As we see already in Heidegger's early work on a work attributed to Duns Scotus, those who want to restore ontology feel themselves largely in agreement with Hegel, namely with respect to an overall conception of Western metaphysics that they hope to get free of later, and in fact in Hegel the extremes of idealism do indeed transcend mere subjectivity, the delusory sphere of philosophical immanence. To apply an expression of Emil Lask's to something more general, in Hegel too, idealism's intention points beyond itself. But behind this formal consonance with the ontological impulse are hidden differences whose subtlety makes all the difference in the world. The Idea, which in Hegel is actually directed against traditional idealism, is not the idea of being but the idea of truth. "That the form of thought is the perfect form, and that it presents the truth as it intrinsically and actually is, is the general dogma of philosophy."[26] The absoluteness of spirit, as opposed to anything merely finite, is intended to vouch for the absoluteness of truth, which is removed from mere opining, from all intention, from all subjective "facts of consciousness"; this is the apex of Hegel's philosophy. For him truth is not a mere relationship between judgment and objects, not a predicate of subjective thought; rather, it is intended to rise substantially above that, indeed, as something "in and for itself," knowing truth is for him nothing less than knowing the absolute: this is the intent of his critique of Kant's critical philosophy with its delimitations and its irreconcilable separation of subjectivity and being-in-itself. In a passage cited by Kroner, Hegel says that Kant's "so-called critical philosophy" has "soothed the conscience of ignorance of the eternal and divine by having proved that nothing can be known of the eternal and divine. . . . Nothing is more welcome to superficiality of knowledge and character, nothing seized upon more readily than this doctrine of ignorance, in which this superficiality and shallowness is presented as excellence, as the aim and result of all intellectual endeavor."[27] This kind of emphatic idea of truth gives the lie to subjectivism, whose assiduous concern with whether truth is true enough terminates in the abolition of truth. The content of consciousness that develops into truth is not truth merely for the knowing subject, whether that subject be a transcendental one or not. The idea of the objectivity of truth strengthens the subject's reason: it is to be possible, attainable for him; current attempts to break out of subjectivism, in contrast, are allied to a defamation of the subject. As an idea of reason, however, Hegel's Idea is distinguished from the restoration of the absolute concept of being by being mediated within itself. For Hegel truth in itself is not "being"; it is precisely in being that abstraction, the approach of the subject that produces its concepts nominalistically, is hidden. In Hegel's idea of truth, however, the subjective moment, the moment of relativity, is surpassed in that it becomes aware of itself. The idea is contained in what is true, although it is not identical with it; "reason is, therefore, misunderstood when reflection is excluded from the True, and is not grasped as a positive moment of the absolute."[28] Perhaps nothing says more about the nature of dialectical thought than that self-consciousness of the subjective moment in truth, reflection on reflection, is to effect a reconciliation with the injustice that the operating subjectivity does to immanent truth in merely supposing and positing as true something that is never wholly true. If the idealist dialectic turns against idealism, it does so because its own principle, because the very overextension of its idealist claim, is at the same time anti-idealist. The dialectic is a process in terms of the immanence of truth as much as in terms of the activity of consciousness: process, that is, is truth itself. Hegel emphasizes this in one formulation after another: "Truth is its own self-movement, whereas the method just described is the mode of cognition that remains external to its material."[29] This movement is elicited by the subject in the activity of thinking: "In my view . . . everything turns on grasping and expressing the True, not only as Substance, but equally as Subject."[30] But because the material that every individual judgment is concerned with is confronted with its concept in that judgment and because every individual, finite judgment disintegrates as untrue in that process, the subjective activity of reflection leads truth out beyond the traditional concept of the adaptation of the idea to its subject matter: truth can no longer be apprehended as a quality characterizing judgments. In Hegel truth is called, as in the traditional definition yet in secret opposition to it, "agreement of the concept with its actuality";[31] it consists in "the coincidence of the object with itself, that is, with its concept."[32] Because, however, no finite judgment ever attains that agreement, the concept of truth is torn loose from predicative logic and transposed into the dialectic as a whole. It is necessary, says Hegel, "to discard the prejudice that truth must be something tangible."[33] Hegel's critique of the rigid separation of the moments of the judgment fuses truth, insofar as it is conceived as mere result, with process. It destroys the illusion that truth could consist in consciousness's measuring itself in terms of some individual thing confronting it:

'True' and 'false' belong among those determinate notions which are held to be inert and wholly separate essences, one here and one there, each standing fixed and isolated from the other, with which it has nothing in common. Against this view it must be maintained that truth is not a minted coin that can be given and pocketed ready-made. Nor is there such a thing as the false, any more than there *is* something evil. . . . To know something falsely means that there is a disparity between knowledge and its Substance. But this very disparity is the process of distinguishing in general, which is an essential moment [in knowing]. Out of this distinguishing, of course, comes their identity, and this resultant identity is the truth. But it is not truth as if the disparity had been thrown away, like dross from pure metal, not even like the tool which remains separate from the finished vessel; disparity, rather, as the negative, the self, is itself still directly present in the True as such.[34]

Hegel breaks here with the doctrine of truth as an *adaequatio rei atque cogitationis,* a doctrine parroted by the whole of philosophy. Through the dialectic, which is the approach of a consistent nominalism awakened to self-consciousness, an approach that examines any and every concept in terms of its subject matter and in doing so convicts it of its inadequacy, a Platonic idea of truth is adumbrated. This idea is not asserted as something obvious and directly present to the intuition; instead, it is aroused in anticipation by the very insistence of intellectual labor, which customarily stops with the critique of Platonism: philosophical reason too has its cunning. Only when the demand for truth refuses to honor the nevertheless inescapable claim to truth made in each and every limited and therefore untrue judgment, a claim that at the same time cannot be dispensed with, only when it negates the subjective *adaequatio* through self-reflection, does truth make the transition of its own accord into an objective idea, an idea that is no longer nominalistically reducible. Hegel also always interprets the movement that is supposed to be truth as "self-movement" [*Eigenbewegung*] that is motivated as much by the state of affairs with which the judgment is concerned as by the synthesis effected by thought. That the subject may not simply content itself with the mere adequacy of its judgments to the states of affairs judged derives from the fact that judgment is not a mere subjective activity, that truth itself is not a mere quality of judgment; rather, in truth something always prevails that, although it cannot be isolated, cannot be reduced to the subject, something that traditional idealist epistemologies believe they can neglect as a mere unknown. Truth divests itself of its subjectivity: because no subjective judgment can be true and yet each and every one must want to be true, truth transcends itself and becomes something in-itself. As something that makes the transition in this way, however, something that is not merely "posited" any more than it is something merely "revealed," truth is also incompatible with what ontology hopes to discover through its inquiries. Hegel's truth is no longer in time, as nominalist truth was, nor is it above time in the ontological fashion: for Hegel time becomes a moment of truth itself. Truth as process is a "passage through *all* moments" as opposed to a "proposition that contains contradictions," and as such it has a temporal core. This liquidates the hypostasis of abstraction and the self-identical concept that dominates traditional philosophy. If Hegel's "movement of the concept" restores Platonism in a certain sense, this Platonism is nevertheless healed of its static quality, its mythic heritage, and has absorbed into itself all the spontaneity of liberated consciousness. Despite everything, Hegel ultimately remains tied to the identity thesis and therefore to idealism, but at a moment in the history of spirit when conformity chains spirit in a way that was not the case a hundred years ago, the now cheap critique of idealism that at that time had to be won from the superior power of idealism needs to be reminded that there is a moment of truth in the identity thesis itself. If, in Kantian terms, there were no similarity between subject and object, if the two, as an unrestrained positivism would have it, stood in absolute and unmediated opposition to one another, then not *only* would there be no truth, there would be no reason and no ideas at all. Thought that completely extirpated its mimetic impulse— the kind of enlightenment that does not carry out the self-reflection that forms the content of the Hegelian system, naming the relationship of the matter at hand to the idea—would end up in madness. Thought that is absolutely without reference—the complete opposite of the philosophy of identity—thought that removes all participation on the subject's part and all anthropomorphism from the object, is the consciousness of the schizophrenic. Its objectivity celebrates its triumph in a pathos-filled narcissism. The speculative Hegelian concept rescues mimesis through spirit's self-reflection: truth is not *adaequatio* but affinity, and in the decline of idealism reason's mindfulness of its mimetic nature is revealed by Hegel to be its human right.

Here one could object that in hypostatizing spirit Hegel, the Platonic realist and absolute idealist, indulged in the same conceptual fetishism that occurs in the name of being today. But a judgment that invoked this similarity would itself remain abstract. Even if abstract thought and abstract being are the same, as an admittedly disputed line from a poem by Parmenides claimed at the beginning of Western philosophy, the ontological concept of being has a different status than the Hegelian concept of reason. Both categories participate in the dynamic of history. Some people, Kroner included, have tried to list Hegel among the irrationalists on the basis of his critique of finite and limited reflection, and there are statements by Hegel that can be adduced to support that argument, such as his statement that speculation, like unmediated belief, stands opposed to reflection. But like Kant in the three critiques, Hegel maintains decisively that reason is one, that it is reason, *ratio*, thought. Even the movement that is to lead out beyond all finite conceptual determinations is a self-critical movement on the part of thought: the speculative concept is neither intuition nor "categorial intuition." The rigor of Hegel's attempt to rescue the ontological proof of God in opposition to Kant may be questioned. But what impelled him to it was not a desire to eclipse reason but on the contrary the utopian hope that the block, the "limits of the possibility of experience," might not be final; that success might be achieved anyway, as in the concluding scene of *Faust:* that spirit, in all its weakness, limitations, and negativity, resembles truth and is therefore suited for knowledge of truth. If at one time the arrogance of the Hegelian doctrine of absolute spirit was

rightly emphasized, today, when idealism is defamed by everyone and most of all by the secret idealists, a wholesome corrective becomes apparent in the notion of spirit's absoluteness. It
passes judgment on the paralyzing resignation in contemporary
consciousness, which, out of its own weakness, is ever ready to
support the degradation done to it by the superior force of blind
existence. "In the so-called 'ontological' proof of the existence of
God, we have the same conversion of the absolute concept into
existence. This conversion has constituted the depth of the Idea
in the modern world, although recently it has been declared
inconceivable, with the result that knowledge of truth has
been renounced, since truth is simply the unity of concept and
existence."[35]

If Hegelian reason resists being merely subjective and negative, and repeatedly functions as spokesperson for what is opposed to this subjective reason, even unearthing the rational in
the irrational with gusto, Hegel does not simply compel the obe-
dience of one who would rebel against this by making the het-
eronomous and estranged appetizing, as though it were reason's
natural subject matter; nor does he merely warn that it is no use
opposing what cannot be changed. Rather, in his innermost core
Hegel sensed that the nature and destiny of human beings can
be realized only through what is estranged, only through the
world's domination, as it were, of human beings. Human beings
must appropriate even the powers that are hostile to them; they
must insinuate themselves into them, so to speak. Hegel intro-
duced the cunning of reason into the philosophy of history in
order to provide a plausible demonstration of the way objective
reason, the realization of freedom, succeeds by means of the blind,
irrational passions of historical individuals. This concept reveals
something about the experiential core of Hegel's thought. His
thought as a whole is cunning; it hopes to achieve victory over

the superior power of the world, about which it has no illusions, by turning this superior power against itself until it turns into something different. In a conversation with Goethe, handed down by Eckermann, in which he was unusually candid, Hegel defined the dialectic as the organized spirit of contradiction. That kind of cunning is not an insubstantial element in the dialectic, a kind of grandiose peasant shrewdness that has learned to submit to the powerful and adapt to their needs until it can wrest their power from them: the dialectic of lordship and bondage lets that secret out. We know that throughout his life Hegel held to the Swabian dialect, even as an ostensible Prussian state philosopher, and reports about him repeatedly note with amazement the surprising simplicity of the character of this man who was so exceptionally difficult as a writer. He remained unfalteringly faithful to his origins, the precondition for a strong ego and any elevation of thought. Of course there is a residue of false positivity in this: Hegel focuses on the circumstances in which he finds himself, like the person who believes he will reaffirm his value by letting one know, through gestures or words, that he is an unimportant man. But that naiveté of the unnaive, whose analogue in the system is the restoration of immediacy at all its levels, itself testifies to an ingenious craftiness, especially in contrast to the stupid, perfidious reproach of artificiality and exaggeration that has been blabbered against every dialectical idea since then. In the naiveté of the idea that is so close to its object that it is on intimate terms with it, as it were, the otherwise so grown-up Hegel preserved, as Horkheimer said, an element of childhood, the courage to be weak that gives the child the idea that it will ultimately overcome even what is most difficult.

In this regard too, of course, Hegel's philosophy, perhaps more dialectical than it itself imagined, walks a narrow line. For as little as it is willing to "renounce knowledge of truth," its tendency to resignation is undeniable. It would like to justify what exists as rational and dispense with the reflection that opposes this, with a superior attitude that boasts about how difficult the world is and draws the moral that it cannot be changed. If anywhere, it is here that Hegel was bourgeois. But to sit in judgment on him even in this regard would be a sign of a servile attitude. The most questionable, and therefore also the best known of Hegel's teachings, that what is real is rational, was not merely apologetic. Rather, in Hegel reason finds itself constellated with freedom. Freedom and reason are nonsense without one another. The real can be considered rational only insofar as the idea of freedom, that is, human beings' genuine self-determination, shines through it. Anyone who tries to conjure away this legacy of the Enlightenment in Hegel and campaign for the idea that his *Logic* has nothing to do with a rational ordering of the world falsifies him. Even where, in his later period, Hegel defends the positive—that which simply is—that he attacked in his youth, he appeals to reason, which understands what merely exists as more than merely existing, understands it from the point of view of self-consciousness and the self-emancipation of human beings. One cannot remove the objective concept of reason from absolute idealism, any more than one can remove its subjective origins in the self-preserving reason of the individual; even in Kant's philosophy of history, self-preservation turns, by virtue of its own movement, into objectivity, into "humanity," into a true society. This alone enabled Hegel to define subjective reason, a necessary moment in absolute spirit, as something universal as well. Even if it does not know it, the reason of the individual, with which, in the dialectic of sense certainty, Hegel's movement of the concept begins, is always already potentially the reason of the species. This much is true even in the otherwise false doctrine of the idealists that sets up transcendental consciousness, which is an abstraction from individual consciousness, as substantial and immanent despite its genetic and logical dependence on individual consciousness. The Janus character of Hegel's philosophy becomes particularly obvious in the category of the individual. Hegel sees through the moment of illusion in individuation as well as his antipode Schopenhauer does—the obstinacy of dwelling on what one merely is oneself, the narrowness and particularity of individual interests. Nevertheless Hegel did not dispossess objectivity or essence of their relationship to the individual and the immediate. The universal is always also the particular and the particular the universal. By analyzing this relationship, the dialectic gives an account of the social force field in which everything individual is socially preformed from the outset and at the same time nothing is realized except in and through individuals. The categories of the particular and the general, the individual and society, cannot be put to rest any more than can those of subject and object, nor can the process that takes place between them be interpreted as a process between two poles that retain their individual identities: the contributions of the two moments—indeed, what those moments actually are—can be discerned only in historical concretion. If nevertheless in the construction of Hegelian philosophy the universal, the substantial, as opposed to the frailty and weakness of the individual, and ultimately the institutional are most strongly accentuated, this expresses more than a complicity with the course of the world, more than the cheap consolation for the fragility of existence that reminds it that it simply is fragile. While Hegel's philosophy draws the full consequences from bourgeois subjectivism, that is, it actually understands the world as a whole as the product of labor—as commodity, if one will, at the same time Hegel gives an extremely sharp critique of subjectivity, one that goes far beyond Fichte's distinction between the subject and the individual. In Hegel, the not-I, which in Fichte was abstractly posited, is developed, subjected to the dialectic, concretely, and hence not only in general terms but in its full specific content, thus serving to delimit the subject. Whereas Heine, surely not the least judicious of Hegel's listeners, could understand Hegel's teachings primarily as a validation of individuality, individuality itself finds itself dealt with roughly, even with contempt, at numerous levels of the system. But this reflects the ambiguity of civil society, which truly attained self-consciousness in Hegel, when it comes to individuality. To civil society, the human being, as unrestrained producer, appears to be autonomous, heir of the divine legislator, virtually omnipotent. For this reason, however, the particular individual, who in this society is truly a mere agent of the social process of production and whose own needs are merely ground down, so to speak, in the process, is also considered completely impotent and insignificant at the same time. In unresolved opposition to the pathos of humanism, Hegel explicitly and implicitly orders human beings, as those who perform socially necessary labor, to subject themselves to an alien necessity. He thereby embodies, in theoretical form, the antinomy of the universal and the particular in bourgeois society. But by formulating it ruthlessly, he makes this antinomy more intelligible than ever before and criticizes it even as he defends it. Because freedom would be the freedom of real, particular individuals, Hegel disdains the illusion of freedom, the individual who, in the midst of universal unfreedom, behaves as though he were already free and universal. Hegel's confidence that theoretical reason can still achieve its goals amounts to the knowledge that reason has a hope of realizing itself, of becoming a rational reality, only if it indicates the pivotal point from which one can dislodge the age-old burden of myth. The burden is mere existence, which in the last analysis entrenches itself in the individual; its pivot point is reason, as the reason of existence itself. Hegel's apologetics and his resignation are the bourgeois mask that utopia has put on to avoid being immediately recognized and apprehended; to avoid remaining impotent.

How little Hegel's philosophy can be reduced to bourgeois civility is perhaps most obvious in his stance on morality. It is a moment in his critique of the category of individuality as such. He was probably the first to express, in the *Phenomenology,* the idea that the rift between self and world passes in turn through the self; that it continues, as Kroner says, on into the individual and divides him in accordance with the objective and subjective rationality of his will and his deeds.[36] Hegel knew early on that the individual himself is both something socially functioning, something defined by the matter at hand, namely, by his labor, and also something that exists for itself, with specific inclinations, interests, and talents, and that these two moments point in different directions. But the purely moral action in which the individual thinks he is himself and only himself, acting autonomously, thereby becomes ambiguous, a self-deception. Modern analytical psychology's recognition that what the individual human being thinks about himself is illusory and to a large extent mere "rationalization" has provided a home for one piece of Hegelian speculation. Hegel derived the transition from pure moral self-consciousness to hypocrisy—which then became the focus of Nietzsche's critical attack on philosophy—from its moment of objective untruth. Historically, of course, formulations like the one in the *Phenomenology* about the "hard heart" that insists on the purity of the moral commandment still fall within the context of the post-Kantian Schillerian critique of rigorous Kantian ethics, but at the same time they represent a prelude to Nietzsche's notion of *ressentiment,* of morality as "revenge." Hegel's statement that there is nothing morally real is not a mere moment in the transition to his notion of concrete ethical life [*Sittlichkeit*]. In it the recognition that the moral can by no means be taken for granted, that conscience does not guarantee right action, and that pure immersion of the self in the question of what to do and what not to do entangles one in contradiction and futility. Hegel takes an impulse of the radical Enlightenment farther. He does not oppose the good to empirical life as an abstract principle, a self-sufficient idea, but instead links it through its own content to the production of a true totality—to precisely what appears under the name of humanity in the *Critique of Practical Reason*. Hegel thereby transcends the bourgeois separation of ethos, as something that although unconditionally binding is valid only for the subject, from the objectivity of society, which is ostensibly merely empirical. This is one of the most remarkable perspectives provided by Hegel's mediation of the a priori and the a posteriori. The incisiveness of his formulation takes us by surprise:

The designation of an individual as immoral *necessarily* falls away when morality in general is imperfect, and has therefore only an arbitrary basis. Therefore, the sense and content of the judgement of experience is solely this, that happiness simply as such should not have been the lot of some individuals, i.e. the judgment is an expression of *envy* which covers itself with the cloak of morality. The reason, however, why so-called good luck should fall to the lot of others, is good friendship, which *grants* and *wishes* them, and itself, too, this lucky chance.[37]

No mere bourgeois would have talked this way. The bourgeois glorification of what exists is always accompanied by the delusion that the individual—that which exists purely for itself, which is how the subject necessarily appears to himself in the existing order—is capable of the good. Hegel destroyed this illusion. His critique of morality cannot be reconciled with that apology for society, which needs a moral ideology of the individual and his renunciation of happiness to sustain itself in its own injustice.

Once one has seen through the cliché of Hegel's bourgeois civility, one will no longer succumb to the suggestion made by Schopenhauer and then Kierkegaard, who dismiss Hegel as a person as conformist and insignificant and derive their negative verdict on his philosophy not least from that. To Hegel's credit, he was not an existential thinker in the sense that was inaugurated by Kierkegaard and has now degenerated to a self-satisfied cliché. The fact that the most recent—and already threadbare—version of the cult of personality does not fit him does not degrade Hegel to the comfortable professor lecturing, unconcerned, on the sufferings of mankind, the picture with which Kierkegaard and Schopenhauer so successfully defamed him to posterity. In fact, Schopenhauer showed infinitely less humanity and generosity to Hegel than the older man had shown him; Hegel granted Schopenhauer his *Habilitation* despite the fact that Schopenhauer, in a foolish debate, had arrogantly played himself off against Hegel as a high-principled researcher who was expert in the natural sciences. Hegel's critique had gone beyond the notion of existence that opposed him long before existence, man the philosopher and his authenticity, had begun to give itself airs and then become established in academia as well. Just as the empirical person who thinks lags behind the power and objectivity of the idea he thinks whenever the idea *is* an idea, an idea's claim to truth does not lie in its adequacy as an illustration of the thinker, in the paltry repetition of what he is anyway. But rather, this claim is proven in that which goes beyond entanglement in mere existence, in that in which the individual human being divests himself of himself so that he may finally reach his goal. Hegel's demeanor, full of suffering, his countenance ravaged by thought, the face of one who has literally consumed himself until he is no more than ashes, bear witness to this self-divestiture. Hegel's bourgeois unpretentiousness worked to the benefit of his immeasurable efforts, inscribed with their own impossibility, to think the unconditioned—an impossibility that Hegel's philosophy reflects within itself as the epitome of negativity. In the face of that, the appeal to authenticity, risk, and the boundary situation is a modest one. If there is truly a need for the thinking subject in philosophy, if there can be no insight into the objectivity of the matter at hand without the element currently dealt with under the trademark of the existential, that moment achieves legitimacy not in showing off but in shattering that self-positing through the discipline imposed on it by the thing itself and extinguishing itself within it. Hegel is almost without peer in following this path. But as soon as the existential moment asserts itself to be the basis of truth, it becomes a lie. Hegel's hatred of those who ascribed the right of full truth to the immediacy of their experience is directed to this lie as well.

The wealth of experience on which thought feeds in Hegel is incomparable; it is put into the ideas themselves, never appearing as mere "material," to say nothing of example or evidence external to the ideas. Through what is experienced, the abstract idea is transformed back into something living, just as mere material is transformed through the path thought travels: one could show this in every sentence of the *Phenomenology of Spirit.* Hegel was in fact granted something praised, usually without justification, in artists: sublimation; he truly possessed life in its colored reflection, in its recapitulation in spirit. But under no circumstances should one conceive sublimation in Hegel as equivalent to internalization. Hegel's conception of self-divestiture, like the critique of a "vain" and deluded subjectivity existing for itself, a critique he shares with Goethe and which moves out beyond idealism, is the opposite of internalization, and as a person Hegel shows hardly a trace of it. Like the subject of his theories, the man Hegel had absorbed both subject and object into himself in spirit; the life of his spirit is all of life again within itself. Hence Hegel's withdrawal from life should not be confused with the ideology of scholarly renunciation. As sublimated spirit, Hegel the person resounds with the outward and the physical the way great music does: Hegel's philosophy murmurs and rustles. As with his devoted critic, Kierkegaard, one could speak of an "intellectual body" in him. His bride, the Baroness Maria von Tucher, took it amiss when he added these words to a letter she had written to his sister: "From this you can see how happy I can be with her for all the rest of my life, and how happy the attainment of such love, for which I scarcely had any hope left in this world, is making me even now, insofar as happiness is part of the destiny of my life." [38] The whole antiprivate Hegel is in these private words. Later, in *Zarathustra,* the thought in them was given a poeticized form: "Trachte ich denn nach Glück? Ich trachte nach meinem Werke" [Do I covet happiness? I covet my work]. But the almost tradesmanlike dryness and sobriety to which the most extreme pathos shrivels in Hegel gives the idea a dignity it loses when it provides its pathos with a fanfare. The meaning of Hegel's life is tied to the substance of his philosophy. No philosophy was so profoundly rich; none held so unswervingly to the experience to which it had entrusted itself without reservation. Even the marks of its failure were struck by truth itself.

The Experiential Content
of Hegel's Philosophy

I will be dealing here with some models of intellectual experience as it motivates Hegel's philosophy—motivates it objectively, not biographically or psychologically—and makes up its truth content. Initially, the concept of experience will be left undefined: only the presentation can concretize it. The concept is not intended to capture phenomenological "ur-experience"; nor, like the interpretation of Hegel in Heidegger's *Holzwege,* is it intended to get at something ontological, the "Wort des Seins" [word of Being] or the "Sein des Seienden" [Being of beings].[1] According to Hegel himself, nothing of this sort is meant to be extracted from his train of thought. His thought would never have ratified Heidegger's claim that "the new object that arises for consciousness in the course of its formation" is "not just anything that is true, or any particular being, but is the truth of what is true, the Being of beings, the appearance of appearance."[2] Hegel would never have called that experience; instead, for Hegel what experience is concerned with at any particular moment is the animating contradiction of such absolute truth. Nothing can be known "that is not in experience"[3]—including, accordingly, the Being into which existential ontology displaces the ground of what exists and is experienced. In Hegel being and ground are "determinations of reflection" [*Reflexionsbestimmungen*], categories inseparable from the subject, as in Kant. The supposition that experience is a mode of being, something that has presubjectively "been appropriated as event" [*ereignet*] or "been elucidated" [*gelichtet*], is simply incompatible with Hegel's conception of experience as a "dialectical movement which consciousness exercises on itself and which affects both its knowledge and its object" inasmuch as the "new true object issues from it."[4]

Nor, however, does the concept of experience refer to isolated empirical observations that would be processed synthetically in Hegel's philosophy. My theme is the experiential substance *of* Hegel's philosophy, not experiential content *in* Hegel's philosophy. What I have in mind is closer to what Hegel, in the introduction to his *System of Philosophy,* calls the "attitude of thought to objectivity"—the attitude of his own thought. I will try to translate into something as close to contemporary experience as possible what Hegel essentially understood, what he saw about the world, prior to the traditional categories of philosophy, even the Hegelian categories, and their critique. I will not go into the controversy within intellectual history about the relative priority of theological and sociopolitical motifs in Hegel's biography. What I am interested in is not how Hegel subjectively arrived at this or that doctrine but rather, in the Hegelian spirit, the compelling force of the objective phenomena that have been reflected in his philosophy and are sedimented in it. Nor will I be concerned with what has been canonized as Hegel's historical achievement—his conception of the notion of development and its linking with metaphysics, which had been static since Plato and Aristotle—or with those aspects of his work that have been absorbed into the individual scholarly disciplines. My inquiry is concerned with what his philosophy expresses as philosophy, and this has its substance not least of all in the fact that it is not exhausted by the findings of individual disciplines.

It seems timely to appeal to this. The tradition of at least the post-Kantian German Idealism that found its most compelling form in Hegel has faded, and for the most part its terminology seems far removed from us. In general, Hegel's approach stands in oblique relationship to the program of unmediated acceptance of the so-called given as a firm basis of knowledge. Since Hegel's day that program has come almost to be taken for granted, and by no means merely in positivism but also in authentic opponents of positivism like Bergson and Husserl. The less human immediacy is tolerated by the omnipresent mediating mechanisms of exchange, the more fervently a compliant philosophy asserts that it possesses the basis of things in the immediate. This kind of spirit has triumphed over speculation both in the positivistic sciences and in their opponents. It is not that there has been an arbitrary change in styles of thought or philosophical fashions, as aestheticist or psychologist views of the history of philosophy like to portray it. Instead, idealism has been forgotten, or has at least become a mere cultural commodity, both out of compulsion and out of necessity; through the compulsion of critical reflection and out of necessity in the development of a society that has less and less fulfilled Hegel's prognosis that it would become absolute spirit, that it would be rational. Even ideas that were at one time firmly established have a history of their truth and not a mere afterlife; they do not remain inherently indifferent to what befalls them. At the present time Hegelian philosophy, and all dialectical thought, is subject to the paradox that it has been rendered obsolete by science and scholarship while being at the same time more timely than ever in its opposition to them. This paradox must be endured and not concealed under a cry of "back to . . ." or an effort to divide the sheep from the goats within Hegel's philosophy. Whether we have only an academic renaissance of Hegel that it is itself long outdated or whether contemporary consciousness finds in Hegel a truth content whose time is due depends on whether that paradox is endured or not. If one wishes to avoid halfheartedly preserving what people praise as Hegel's sense of reality while at the same time watering down his philosophy, one has no choice but to put the very moments in him that cause consternation into relation to the experiences his philosophy incorporates, even if those experiences are encoded within it and their truth is concealed.

To do so is not to betray Hegel to empiricism but rather to keep faith with his own philosophy, with the desideratum of immanent criticism, which is a central piece in his method. For Hegelian philosophy claims to have gone beyond the opposition between rationalism and empiricism, as beyond all rigid oppositions in the philosophical tradition: it claims both to capture spirit interpretively in its experiences of the world and to construct experience through the movement of spirit. One is only taking his philosophy at its word when one virtually disregards its place in the history of philosophy and reduces it to its experiential core, which should be identical with its spirit. In a passage from the introduction to the *Phenomenology,* cited by Heidegger as well, Hegel himself identifies experience with the dialectic.[5] One may object that it is primarily individual categories and ideas that have been selected and the fully elaborated system is not given immediate consideration, when the system is supposed to be decisive for all the individual elements in it, but Hegel's own intention once again covers the objection. The system is not to be conceived in advance, abstractly; it is not to be an all-encompassing schema. Instead, it is supposed to be the effective center of force latent in the individual moments. They are supposed to crystallize, on their own and by virtue of their motion and direction, into a whole that does not exist outside of its particular determinations. There is no guarantee, of course, that reduction to experiences will confirm the identity of opposites within the whole that is both a presupposition and a result of the Hegelian method. Perhaps the reduction will prove fatal to the claim of identity.

The difficulty specific to beginning should not be minimized. In schools of philosophy that make emphatic use of the concept of experience, in the tradition of Hume, the character of immediacy—immediacy in relation to the subject—is itself the criterion of that concept. Experience is supposed to be something immediately present, immediately given, free, as it were, of any admixture of thought and therefore indubitable. Hegel's philosophy, however, challenges this concept of immediacy, and with it the customary concept of experience. "What is unmediated is often held to be superior, the mediated being thought of as dependent. The concept, however, has both aspects: it is mediation through its sublation of mediation, and so is immediacy."[6] According to Hegel, there is nothing between heaven and earth that is not *"vermittelt"* [mediated], nothing, therefore, that does not contain, merely by being defined as something that exists, the reflection of its mere existence, a spiritual moment: "Immediacy itself is essentially mediated."[7] If Kantian philosophy, which Hegel, for all his polemics, presupposes, tries to tease out the forms of the spirit as constituents of all valid knowledge, then Hegel, in order to do away with the Kantian separation of form and content, interprets any and every existing thing as something that is at the same time spiritual. Not the least significant of Hegel's epistemological findings is the idea that even the elements in which knowledge imagines itself to possess its ultimate and irreducible basis are in turn always the products of abstraction and thereby of "spirit." A simple illustration of this is that the so-called sense impressions to which the older epistemology reduces all knowledge are themselves mere constructions and do not appear as such in pure form in living consciousness; that except in the artificial conditions of the laboratory, estranged from living knowledge, no red at all is perceived from which the so-called higher syntheses would then be composed. Those allegedly elementary qualities of immediacy always appear already categorically formed, and thus the sensory and the categorial moments cannot be clearly distinguished from one another as "layers." "Empiricism is not merely an observing, hearing, feeling, etc., a perception of the individual; for it really sets to work to find the species, the universal, to discover laws. Now because it does this, it comes within the territory of the concept . . ."[8] Hegel's antipositivist insight has been redeemed by modern science only to the extent that Gestalt theory has shown that there is no such thing as an isolated, unqualified sensory "this thing here"; it is always already structured. But Gestalt theory did not upset the primacy of the given, the belief in its precedence over the contribution made by subjectivity, and thereby harmonize knowledge: just as for positivism the given was unmediated, so for Gestalt theory its unity with form is unmediated, a kind of thing in itself amid the immanence of consciousness. That form and givenness, between which classical epistemology made a sharp distinction, are not fully equivalent is only peripherally acknowledged by Gestalt theory, in distinctions like that between the good and the bad Gestalt, which fall within the Gestalt concept that is accepted from the outset. Hegel had already gone far beyond this in the *Phenomenology of Spirit*. He demolished the thesis of mere immediacy as the basis of knowledge and opposed the empiricist concept of experience without glorifying the given as the bearer of meaning. It is characteristic of his method that he evaluated immediacy by its own criterion and charged it with not being immediate. He criticizes immediacy in principle and not merely as being atomistic and mechanical; immediacy always already contains something other than itself—subjectivity—without which it would not be "given" at all, and by that token it is already not objectivity. "This principle of Experience carries with it the unspeakably important condition that, in order to accept and believe any fact, we must be in contact with it; or, in more exact terms, that we must find the fact united and combined with the certainty of our own selves."[9] But Hegel does not simply sacrifice the concept of immediacy; if he did, his own idea of experience would lose its rational meaning. "Immediacy of knowledge is so far from excluding mediation, that the two things are linked together,—immediate knowledge being actually the product and result of mediated knowledge."[10] One can no more speak of mediation without something immediate than, conversely, one can find something immediate that is not mediated. But in Hegel the two moments are no longer rigidly contrasted. They produce and reproduce one another reciprocally, are formed anew at each stage, and are to vanish, reconciled, only in the unity of the whole. "And to show that, in point of fact, there is a knowledge which advances neither by unmixed immediacy nor by unmixed mediation, we can point to the example of Logic and the whole of philosophy."[11] But with this, the intention of deriving Hegel's philosophy from experience seems itself condemned by the verdict it pronounces when it takes Kant's critical philosophy to the extreme. The only "experience" of which it can be a question in and with respect to Hegel alters the usual concept of experience decisively.

It is most difficult to get hold of the experiential content of Hegel's philosophy where it sets itself off from philosophies that take experience as their principle. As we know, Hegel energetically accentuates the moment of not-I in spirit. But to dispute that he is an idealist must remain the prerogative of interpretive arts that follow the maxim "Reim dich oder ich fress dich" [literally, "rhyme or I'll eat you"; in other words, "come out right or there will be trouble"] when they see a chance to exploit the authority of a great name for propaganda purposes. They would have to reduce his statement that truth is essentially subject[12] to an irrelevant statement that in the last analysis would leave no *differentia specifica* in Hegel's system. Instead, one ought to look for the experiential content of Hegelian idealism itself. But that is something he shares with the movement of the post-Kantian systems in Germany as a whole, and especially with Fichte and Schelling. Perhaps under the tenacious suggestion of Dilthey, that period continues to be forced too narrowly into the perspective of individual thinkers and their differences. In actuality, in the decades from Fichte's *Science of Knowledge* to Hegel's death, idealism was less something strictly individuated than a collective movement: in Hegel's terminology, an intellectual atmosphere. The ideas were neither attached exclusively to one system or the other nor always fully articulated by the individual thinker. Even after the split between Schelling and Hegel one finds in both of them—in the *Ages of the World* in Schelling's case, in the *Phenomenology* in Hegel's—formulations and whole trains of thought in which it is just as difficult to identify the author as it was in the writings of their youth. That ought, incidentally, to clear up a number of difficulties. These writers do not operate with fixed concepts in the manner of a later philosophy modeled on the science the idealist generation opposed. The climate of collective agreement permitted one to express one's opinion even when the individual formulation did not achieve complete lucidity; it may even have worked against a concern for incisive formulation, as though such formulation would violate the content of the collective understanding by producing it explicitly. By no means does the experiential content of idealism simply coincide with its epistemological and metaphysical positions. The pathos in the word "spirit," which ultimately made it suspect of hubris, resisted the first symptoms of the type of science—which includes scholarship—that has since seized power even where it supposedly deals with spirit. That impulse can be sensed even in passages like this one from the *Difference Between Fichte's and Schelling's System of Philosophy*, the *Differenzschrift:*

Only so far as reflection has connection with the Absolute is it Reason and its deed a knowing. Through this connection with the Absolute, however, reflection's work passes away; only the connection persists, and it is the sole reality of the cognition. There is therefore no truth in isolated reflection, in pure thinking, save the truth of its nullification. But because in philosophizing the Absolute gets produced by reflection for consciousness, it becomes thereby an objective totality, a whole of knowledge, an organization of cognitions. Within this organization, every part is at the same time the whole; for its standing is its connection with the Absolute. As a part that has other parts outside of it, it is something limited, and is only through the others. Isolated in its limitation the part is defective; meaning and significance it has solely through its coherence with the whole. Hence single concepts by themselves and singular cognitions (*Erkenntnisse*) must not be called knowledge. There can be plenty of singular empirical known items (*Kenntnisse*). As known from experience they exhibit their justification in experience, that is, in the identity of concept and being, of subject and object. Precisely for this reason, they are not scientific knowledge: they find their justification only in a limited, relative identity. They do not justify themselves as necessary parts of a totality of cognitions organized in consciousness, nor has speculation recognized the absolute identity in them, i.e., their connection with the Absolute.[13]

As a critique of the institutionalized science that is as dominant now as it was then, Hegel's total idealism has its timeliness: against something else, not in itself. The impulse to elevate spirit, however deluded, draws its strength from a resistance to dead knowledge: a resistance to the reified consciousness that Hegel both dissolved and, in opposition to romanticism, salvaged as inescapable. The experience of post-Kantian German Idealism reacts against philistine narrowness and contentment with the compartmentalization of life and organized knowledge in accordance with the division of labor. In this regard even seemingly peripheral, practical texts like Fichte's *Deduzierte Plan* and Schelling's *Einleitung ins Akademische Studium* have philosophical import. The watchword "infinity," which flowed so easily from all their pens as it had not from Kant's, takes on its specific coloration only in relation to what were for them the privations of the finite, of entrenched self-interest and the dreary specialization of knowledge in which that self-interest was reflected. Since then, talk about wholeness has been divested of its polemical meaning and has become nothing more than anti-intellectualist ideology. In the early Idealist period, when bourgeois society had not yet really taken shape as a totality in underdeveloped Germany, the critique of the particular had a different kind of dignity. In the theoretical sphere, idealism represented the insight that the sum total of specific knowledge was not a whole, that the best of both knowledge and human potential slipped through the meshes of the division of labor. Goethe's "fehlt nur das geistige Band" ["But the spiritual bond is missing"—*Faust*] gives that sententious formulation. At one time, idealism attacked Faust's famulus Wagner. Only when the likes of that Wagner had inherited idealism did it reveal itself to be the particularity that Hegel had recognized, at least in Fichte. In a total society, totality becomes radical evil. What resonates in Hegel along with the need for a progressive integration is the need for a reconciliation—a reconciliation the totality has prevented ever since it achieved the reality Hegel enthusiastically anticipated for it in the concept.

One does not need the speculative concept to understand this motif in the critique of science: that what lies closest to the individual subject, what has immediate certainty for him, is not the ground of truth and not absolutely certain. The personal consciousness of the individual, which was analyzed by traditional epistemology, can be seen to be illusion. Not only does the bearer of personal consciousness owe his existence and the reproduction of his life to society. In fact, everything through which he is specifically constituted as a cognitive subject, hence, that is, the logical universality that governs his thinking, is, as the school of Durkheim in particular has shown, always also social in nature. The individual, who considers himself the legitimate basis of truth by virtue of what is supposed to be immediately given for him, obeys the web of delusion of a society that falsely but necessarily thinks of itself as individualistic. What the individual holds to be primary and irrefutably absolute is derived and secondary, down to every individual piece of sensory data. "Therefore the individual as he appears in this world of prose and everyday is not active out of the entirety of his own self and his resources, and he is intelligible not from himself, but from something else."[14] Taking as one's point of departure the pure immediacy of the "this thing here," which is presumably what is most certain, does not get one beyond the contingency of the individual person who simply exists, does not get beyond solipsism. As Schopenhauer said, solipsism may be curable, but it is not refutable. This is the price in insanity paid for that web of delusion. A mode of thinking that understands the individual as *zoon politikon* and the categories of subjective consciousness as implicitly social will no longer cling to a notion of experience that hypostatizes the individual, even if involuntarily. Experience's advance to consciousness of its interdependence with the experience of all human beings acts as a retroactive correction to its starting point in mere individual experience. Hegel's philosophy formulated this. His critique of immediacy gives an account of how what naive consciousness trusts as immediate and most intimate is, objectively, no more immediate and primary than any other kind of possession. Hegel destroys the very mythology of something "first": "That which first commences is implicit, immediate, abstract, general—it is what has not yet advanced; the more concrete and richer comes later, and the first is poorer in determinations."[15] Seen in terms of this kind of demythologization, Hegelian philosophy becomes the figure of a comprehensive commitment to a lack of naiveté; an early answer to a state of the world that incessantly participates in weaving its own veil of illusion. "As a matter of fact, thinking is always the negation of what we have immediately before us."[16] Like Schopenhauer, his antipode, Hegel would like to rend the veil: hence his polemic against Kant's doctrine of the unknowability of the thing in itself.[17] This is certainly one of the deepest motives of Hegel's philosophy, even though his philosophy itself is unaware of it.

The layer of thought touched on here is distinguished from Kant and the whole eighteenth century, as is indeed already the case in Fichte, by a new expressive need. Having matured, thought wants to do something it had previously done only unconsciously: it wants to write the history of spirit, to become an echo of the hour that has struck for it. It is this, more than what the official history of philosophy has designated as the difference, that distinguishes German Idealism, and Hegel in particular, from the Enlightenment. This difference is more important even than Enlightenment's self-critique, the emphatic incorporation of the concrete subject and the historical world, or the dynamization of philosophical activity. With Kant, theoretical philosophy at least still drew its canon from the positive sciences with its examination of their validity, that is, the question of how scientific knowledge is possible. Now philosophy turns, with its whole armature of self-reflection on the theory of science, to the task of giving cogent expression to something that is perceived as central in reality but slips through the meshes of the individual disciplines. This, and not a greater abundance of material, is what motivates philosophy's turn to content, the modern climate of Hegel as contrasted with Kant and now Fichte as well. But Hegel did not make philosophy into a consistent intellectual treatment of experiences of reality through spontaneous, unreflected thinking, either in the form of naive-realistic thought or in the form of what is popularly called unbridled speculation. Instead, rather than restrict himself to a propaedeutic examination of epistemological possibilities, he led philosophy to essential insights through critical self-reflection of critical-Enlightenment philosophy and the scientific method. Trained in science and using its methods, Hegel went beyond the limits of a science that merely ascertained and arranged data, a science that aimed at the processing of materials, the kind of science that predominated before Hegel and then again after him, when thought lost the inordinate span of its self-reflection. Hegel's philosophy is both a philosophy of reason and an antipositivist philosophy. It attacks mere epistemology by showing that the forms that epistemology considers to constitute knowledge depend as much on the content of knowledge as vice-versa. "There is no form at all without matter and no matter without form. Matter and form generate each other reciprocally."[18] In order to demonstrate that, however, Hegel himself makes use of a more consistent epistemology. If epistemology, the doctrine of the contingency and impenetrability of content and the indispensability of forms, dug the trench between matter and form, Hegel extends epistemology until it becomes obvious that it is not its place to dig trenches, that in setting limits, consciousness necessarily transcends what it delimits. Canonic for Hegel is Goethe's statement that everything perfect points beyond its own kind—and Hegel has far more in common with Goethe than one might suspect from the superficial difference between the doctrine of the ur-phenomenon and that of a self-moving absolute.

Kant "anchored" philosophy in synthetic a priori judgments; they epitomized, so to speak, what was left of the old metaphysics after the critique of reason. But there is a deep contradiction running through synthetic a priori judgments. If they were a priori in the strict Kantian sense, they would have no content. They would in fact be forms, pure logical propositions, tautologies in which knowledge does not add anything new or different to itself. If, however, they are synthetic, that is, if they are genuine knowledge and not mere reduplications of the subject, then they need the content that Kant wanted to banish from their sphere as contingent and merely empirical. Given this radical discontinuity, how form and content meet and fit together, how the knowledge whose validity Kant wanted to justify is achieved, becomes an enigma. Hegel's response is that form and content are essentially mediated by one another. This means, however, that a merely formal theory of knowledge, such as epistemology sets forth, negates itself; it is not possible. In order to attain the cogency epistemology yearns for, philosophy must break epistemology open. Hence a philosophizing focused on content, one that tries to formulate experiences in their necessity and cogency, is brought about precisely by the self-reflection of a formal philosophizing that had rejected it and prohibited it as dogmatic. With this transition to content, the separation of the a priori from the empirical world, a separation that had been maintained in the whole Platonic-Aristotelian tradition through Kant and was first questioned by Fichte, is abolished: "The empirical, grasped in its synthesis, is the speculative concept."[19] Philosophy acquires the right and accepts the duty to appeal to material moments originating in the real life process of socialized human beings as essential and not merely contingent. The artificially resurrected metaphysics of today, which castigates that as a descent into mere facticity and claims to protect the being of beings from beings, regresses behind Hegel when it comes to what is crucial, no matter how much that metaphysics mistakenly considers itself to be more advanced than his idealism. Because of his idealism, Hegel has been reproached for being abstract in comparison with the concreteness of the phenomenological, anthropological, and ontological schools. But he brought infinitely more concreteness into his philosophical ideas than those approaches, and not because his speculative imagination was balanced by a sense of reality and historical perspective but by virtue of the approach his philosophy takes—by virtue, one might say, of the experiential character of his speculation. Philosophy, Hegel asserts, must come to understand that "its content is no other than actuality. At first we become aware of these contents in what we call Experience."[20] Philosophy refuses to be intimidated, to renounce the hope of coming to know that whole of reality and its contents to which the institution of science and scholarship bars access in the name of valid, water-tight findings. Hegel sensed the regressive and tyrannical moment in Kant's modesty and opposed the famous saying with which Kant's Enlightenment endeared itself to obscurantism: "I have therefore found it necessary to deny knowledge, in order to make room for faith. The dogmatism of metaphysics, that is, the preconception that it is possible to make headway in metaphysics without a previous criticism of pure reason, is the source of all that unbelief, always very dogmatic, which wars against morality."[21] Hegel's antithesis to this reads, "The sealed essence of the universe has no power that could withstand the spirit of knowledge; it is compelled to open itself to it and lay out its riches and its depths and offer them for its enjoyment."[22] In formulations like this, the Baconian pathos of the early bourgeois period is extended to become that of a mature humankind: we may yet succeed. Seen against the resignation of the current era, this impulse establishes Hegel's true contemporary relevance. The extreme of idealism, the criterion by which the early Hegel, like Hölderlin, condemned a spirit pledged to "utility" and thus unfaithful to itself, has its materialist implications. They disappear when this kind of extreme idealism makes an alliance with what was later called realism, when spirit adapts—and of course it was made abundantly clear to spirit that it could not actualize itself except by adapting. The farther Hegel takes idealism, even epistemologically, the closer he comes to social materialism; the more he insists, against Kant, on comprehending his subject matter from the inside out. Spirit's confidence that the world "in itself" is spirit is not only a narrow illusion of its own omnipotence. It feeds on the experience that nothing whatsoever exists outside of what is produced by human beings, that nothing whatsoever is completely independent of social labor. Even nature, seemingly untouched by labor, is defined as nature by labor and to this extent is mediated by it. Such relationships are strikingly evident in the problem of the so-called noncapitalist areas, which according to the theory of imperialism are a function of the capitalist areas: the latter need the former for the valorization of capital. Leibniz's claim to have constructed the world on the basis of its inner principle, a claim that Kant rejected as dogmatic metaphysics, returns in Hegel as its opposite. What exists comes to approximate the product of labor, without, however, the natural moment disappearing within labor. If, as in Hegel, in the totality everything ultimately collapses into the subject as absolute spirit, idealism thereby cancels itself out, because no difference remains through which the subject would be identified as something distinct, as subject. Once the object has become subject in the absolute, the object is no longer inferior vis-à-vis the subject. At its extreme, identity becomes the agent of the nonidentical. While the limits that prevented this step from being taken explicitly were firmly established in Hegel's philosophy, nevertheless the step remains crucial for content of his philosophy. Left-Hegelianism was not a development in intellectual history that went beyond Hegel and distorted him through misunderstanding; true to the dialectic, it was a piece of the self-reflection that his philosophy had to deny itself in order to remain philosophy.

For this reason even the idealist ferment in Hegel should not be hastily dismissed as presumptuousness. It draws its strength from what the so-called prescientific mind sees in science, something science glosses over in its complacency. In order to be able to operate with the clean, clear concepts it brags about, science establishes such concepts and makes its judgments without regard for the fact that the life of the subject matter for which the concept is intended does not exhaust itself in conceptual specification. What furnishes the canon for Hegelian idealism is the resistance to practical, merely verbal definitions shown by a spirit that has not yet been processed and dressed by science, the need to grasp—as the German word *Begriff* [concept, from *greifen,* grasp] implies—what the matter at hand actually is and what essential and by no means mutually harmonious moments it contains, rather than merely manipulating concepts as tokens. That idealism, which is reproached with being unreflectively arrogant, wants to fully disclose the matter at hand through its concept because in the last analysis the thing itself and its concept are one and the same. On the surface it would seem that Hegelian philosophy nowhere distances itself more from the predialectical concept of experience than here: what happens to spirit is ascribed to spirit, rather than spirit simply arranging it, because after all it is nothing but spirit. But even this most anti-empirical point in Hegel's philosophy is not without an object. It registers the distinction between the matter at hand, the object of knowledge, and the scientific copy of it, with which a self-critical science cannot be satisfied. But the concept cannot transcend its own arbitrary nature, which abstracts, classifies, and delimits. Hegel detested attempts to do so—such as, at that time, Schelling's—and with good reason. They betrayed what he cared most about, his dream of the truth of the matter itself, for the sake of an intellectual intuition that does not go beyond the concept but rather falls short of it and, by usurping the objectivity of the concept, regresses to the subjectivity of mere opinion. There is nothing that philosophical thought is more touchy about than something very close to it that compromises it by hiding the difference that makes all the difference in an inconspicuous nuance. Hence Hegel taught that the meanings of concepts are both to be pinned down, *more scientifico,* so that they can remain concepts, and also to be "set in motion," altered according to the dictates of the object, in order not to distort it. The dialectic is expected to elaborate this postulate, which would otherwise be merely paradoxical. Contrary to what it has become, both in parody and in its dogmatic petrification, dialectic does not mean readiness to replace the meaning of one concept with another one illicitly obtained. Not that one is supposed to eliminate the law of contradiction, as seems to be expected of Hegelian logic. Rather, contradiction itself—the contradiction between the fixed concept and the concept in motion—becomes the agent of philosophizing. When the concept is pinned down, that is, when its meaning is confronted with what is encompassed by it, its non-identity—the fact that the concept and the thing itself are not one and the same—becomes evident within the identity of concept and thing that is required by the logical form of definition. Hence the concept that remains true to its own meaning must change; if it is to follow its own conception, a philosophy that holds the concept to be something more than a mere instrument of the intellect must abandon definition, which might hinder it in doing so. The movement of the concept is not a sophistical manipulation that would insert changing meanings into it from the outside but rather the ever-present consciousness of both the identity of and the inevitable difference between the concept and what it is supposed to express, a consciousness that animates all genuine knowledge. Because philosophy will not relinquish that identity, it must accept this difference.

All self-reflection notwithstanding, however, the words "reflection" and *"Reflexionsphilosophie"* [philosophy of reflection] and their synonyms often have a derogatory tone in Hegel. Nevertheless, his critique of reflection, in which even Fichte was not spared, was itself reflection. This is strikingly evident in the splitting of the concept of the subject that distinguishes him and his speculative-idealist predecessors so drastically from Kant. In Kant, philosophy was engaged in the critique of reason; a somewhat naive scientific consciousness, assessment in terms of the rules of logic—what is currently called "phenomenology"—was applied to consciousness as a condition of knowledge. In Hegel the relationship between the two, between the philosophical, critical consciousness and the consciousness engaged in direct knowledge of its object, the consciousness that is the object of criticism, a relationship that Kant did not consider, becomes thematic, the object of reflection. In the process, consciousness as object, as something to be grasped philosophically, becomes the finite, limited, and fallible thing it had already tended to be conceived as in Kant, who because of this finiteness forbade consciousness to wander off into intelligible worlds. Kant's delimitation of consciousness as a scientific consciousness that makes straightforward judgments returns in Hegel as the negativity of consciousness, as something that needs to be criticized. Conversely, the consciousness that grasps the finiteness of consciousness, the contemplating subjectivity that "posits" the contemplated subject, also thereby posits itself as infinite and—or so is Hegel's intention—when his philosophy is fully elaborated, proves itself in its infiniteness to be absolute spirit, to which nothing is external and in which the difference between subject and object disappears. However dubious this claim may be, the reflection of reflection, the doubling of philosophical consciousness, is no mere play of thought unleashed and as it were divested of its material; it is sound. In that consciousness recalls, through self-reflection, how it has failed to capture reality, how it has mutilated things with its ordering concepts and reduced them to the contingent status of what is closest to hand in its "data," scientific consciousness comes face to face in Hegel with what a causal-mechanistic science, as a science of the domination of nature, has done to nature. In this Hegel was not so different from Bergson, who like him used epistemological analysis to expose the inadequacy of a narrow-minded, reifying science, its lack of congruence with reality—while unreflective science loves to rant and rave about consciousness of this inadequacy being mere metaphysics. Granted, in Bergson the critique of the scientific spirit was carried out by the scientific spirit without much concern for the contradiction in this self-criticism. This is why Bergson could be a theorist of knowledge and an irrationalist at the same time: his philosophy did not successfully come to terms with the relationships of the two aspects. Hegel, a hundred years older, did. He knew that any critique of a reifying, divisive, alienating consciousness that merely sets up a different source of knowledge from the outside as a contrast to it is impotent; that a conception of reason that supersedes reason must fail hopelessly by its own criteria. Hence Hegel made the contradiction between the scientific spirit and the critique of science, which in Bergson is an unmediated contradiction, the motor of philosophical activity. Only through reflection can reflective thought get beyond itself. Contradiction, proscribed by logic, becomes an organ of thought: of the truth of Logos.

Hegel's critique of *Wissenschaft* [science and scholarship], a word he uses repeatedly and with emphasis, is not intended to be an apologetic restoration of pre-Kantian metaphysics as opposed to the scientific thought that has snatched more and more of its subject matter and theories from it. Hegel has a thoroughly rational objection to rational science: that rational science, which imagines itself to be the basis of truth's legitimacy, trims objects down to size and processes them until they fit into the institutionalized, "positive" disciplines, and does so in the service of its own ordering concepts and their immanent practicability and lack of contradiction. What motivates Hegel's concept of reification is the idea that science is concerned less with the life of things that with their compatibility with its own rules: what acts as though it were irreproachable, irreducible truth is itself a product of a preliminary processing, something secondary and derivative. Not the least of the tasks of philosophical consciousness is that of dissolving, through self-reflection, what has become congealed and frozen through science, returning it to what science has removed it from. The very objectivity of science is merely subjective: Hegel's objection to the unreflective labor of the intellect is as rational as his corrective to it. The critique of the institution of positivist science, which increasingly presents itself the world over as the sole legitimate form of knowledge, is already fully developed in Hegel. Long before matters had gone so far, Hegel had recognized it for what it has now, in innumerable dull and empty studies, revealed itself to be—the unity of reification, that is, of a false—in Hegel's terms, abstract—objectivity external to the thing itself, and a naiveté that confuses facts and figures, the plaster model of the world, with its foundation.

Using the language of epistemology and the language of speculative metaphysics extrapolated from it, Hegel expressed the idea that the reified and rationalized society of the bourgeois era, the society in which a nature-dominating reason had come to fruition, could become a society worthy of human beings— not by regressing to older, irrational stages prior to the division of labor but only by applying its rationality to itself, in other words, only through a healing awareness of the marks of unreason in its own reason, and the traces of the rational in the irrational as well. Since then the element of unreason has become evident in the consequences of modern rationality, which threaten universal catastrophe. In *Parsifal* Richard Wagner, the Schopenhauerian, put Hegel's experience in terms of the ancient topos: only the spear that inflicted the wound can heal it. Hegel's philosophical consciousness suffered more from the estrangement between subject and object, between consciousness and reality, than had any previous philosophical consciousness. But his philosophy had the strength not to flee from this suffering back into the chimera of a world and a subject of pure immediacy. It did not let itself be distracted from its awareness that only through the realized truth of the whole would the unreason of a merely particular reason, that is, a reason that merely serves particular interests, disintegrate. This says more about his reflection of reflection than the irrationalist gestures into which Hegel sometimes let himself be misled in his desperate attempts to rescue the truth of a society that had already become untrue. Hegel's self-reflection of the subject in philosophical consciousness is actually society's dawning critical consciousness of itself.

The motif of contradiction, and with it that of a reality that confronts the subject as harsh, alien, and coercive—a motif in which Hegel anticipated Bergson, the metaphysician of flow—is generally considered the over-arching principle of Hegel's philosophy. It is the basis of the dialectical method. But it is precisely this principle that requires translation into the intellectual experience it expresses. It very easily congeals to become the trademark of a view, formulated solely in terms of the history of philosophy, that subsumes the stages of spirit under binding higher-level concepts. The dialectic is reduced to the kind of elective weltanschauung against which the critical philosophy of which Hegel was a part directed such a devastating critique. Hence one cannot evade the question of what justified Hegel in subjecting everything that confronted thought, as well as thought itself, to the principle of contradiction. It is especially at this point in Hegel, who wanted to surrender to the movement of the matter at hand and cure thought of its arbitrariness, that one suspects him of a moment of arbitrariness, of the old dogmatism—and in fact speculative philosophy since Salomon Maimon has in many respects fallen back upon pre-Kantian rationalism. The fact that Hegel expressed the most cutting objections to the claptrap scheme of a triplicity of thesis, antithesis, and synthesis as a mere methodological schema, and that he says in the preface to the *Phenomenology* that as long as it remains a schema, that is, is merely impressed upon objects from the outside, one acquires the "knack" quickly,[23] is not sufficient to allay this suspicion. Nor is one likely to be satisfied with the statement that no isolated principle, whether it be that of mediation, of becoming, of contradiction, or of the dialectic itself, is, as a separate principle, absolute and the key to the truth; that truth consists solely in the relationship of moments that emerge from one another. All that could be mere assertion. Suspicion of the dialectic as an isolated, "abstractly" posited maxim, as Hegel puts it, currently receives confirmation from the way the Hegelian-derived materialist version of the dialectic, of dynamic thought κατ᾽ ἐξοχήν, has been distorted in the Eastern zone, in the abominable abbreviation Diamat, to a literal, static dogma. Now as then, appeal to its inaugurators, who have been degraded to the status of classics, prevents any objective reflection, calling it objectivist deviation; in Diamat, Hegel's movement of the concept has been frozen into an article of faith. By contrast, something that Nietzsche expressed long after Hegel has more in common with the experience that motivates the dialectic: "There is nothing in reality that would correspond strictly with logic."[24] But Hegel did not simply proclaim that; he achieved it, through immanent criticism of logic and its forms. He demonstrated that concept, judgment, and conclusion, unavoidable instruments for ascertaining through consciousness something that exists, always end up contradicting that existing thing; that all individual judgments, all individual concepts, all individual conclusions, are false by the criterion of an emphatic idea of truth. In this way Kant, the mortal enemy of a merely "rhapsodistic" thought that absolutizes contingent individual definitions, came into his own in Hegel, his critic. Hegel attacks the Kantian doctrine of the limits of knowledge and yet respects it. From it he develops the theory of a difference between subject and object that manifests itself in every particular. This difference, which acts as its own corrective, moves out beyond itself to become more adequate knowledge. Accordingly, the justification of the primacy of negation in Hegel's philosophy is that the limits of knowledge to which its critical self-reflection leads are not something external to knowledge, not something to which it is merely condemned from the outside; rather, they are inherent in all moments of knowledge. All knowledge, and not merely knowledge that ventures out into the infinite, aims, through the mere form of the copula, at the whole truth, and none achieves it. Hence in Hegel the Kantian limits of knowledge become the principle of epistemological advance. "A thing is what it is, only in and by reason of its limit. We cannot therefore regard the limit as only external to being which is then and there. It rather goes through and through the whole of such existence."[25] The universality of negation is not a metaphysical panacea that is supposed to open all doors but merely the consequence of the critique of knowledge, now matured to self-awareness, that demolished panaceas. In other words, Hegel's philosophy is eminently critical philosophy, and the examination to which it subjects its concepts, beginning with that of being, always accumulates within itself, like an electrical charge, the specific objections that can be made to it. Of all the distortions perpetrated on Hegel by a dim-witted intelligentsia, the most pitiful is the notion that the dialectic has to admit as valid either everything whatsoever or nothing whatsoever. In Kant, critique remains a critique of reason; in Hegel, who criticizes the Kantian separation of reason from reality, the critique of reason is simultaneously a critique of the real. The inadequacy of all isolated particular definitions is always also the inadequacy of the particular reality that is grasped in those definitions. Even if the system ultimately equates reason and reality and subject and object, the dialectic turns its polemic against the irrationality of mere existence, the enduring state of nature, by confronting a specific reality with its own concept, its own rationality. As long as it remains unreconciled and not yet fully rational, reality reveals itself to be a reality pledged to death. With the concept of determinate negation, which sets Hegel off from Nietzsche's statement as well as from all irrationalism, Hegel does more than merely oppose abstract subsumptive concepts, including that of negation itself. For at the same time negation intervenes in the reality that is the content of the self-criticizing concept: society. "One thing may be observed with reference to the immediate knowledge of God, of legal and ethical principles": they "are still on every side conditioned by the mediating process which is termed development, education, training."[26]

Dialectical contradiction is experienced in the experience of society. Hegel's own construction, formulated in terms of the philosophy of identity, requires that contradiction be grasped as much from the side of the object as from the side of the subject; it is in the dialectical contradiction that there crystallizes a concept of experience that points beyond absolute idealism. It is the concept of antagonistic totality. Just as the principle of universal mediation, as opposed to the immediacy of the mere subject, goes back to the fact that in all categories of thought the objectivity of the social process is prior to the contingency of the individual subject, so the metaphysical conception of a reconciled whole as the quintessence of all contradictions is based on the model of a society that is divided and nevertheless united. Truly a model of society, for Hegel is not content with the general concept of an antagonistic reality, the notion of ur-polarities of being, for instance. In the *Phenomenology of Spirit*, taking as his critical point of departure what is closest to hand, unmediated human consciousness, he accomplishes the mediation of that consciousness in and through the historical movement of what exists, a movement that takes it beyond all mere metaphysics of being. Once set in motion, the concretization of philosophy cannot be stopped for the sake of philosophy's illusory dignity. "It is part of the cowardice of abstract thought that it shuns the sensuous present in a monkish fashion; modern abstraction takes up this attitude of fastidious gentility towards the moment of the sensuous present."[27] That concreteness enables Hegel to completely permeate the idea of totality, which is derived from the idealist system, with the idea of contradiction. Deciphered, the logical-metaphysical theory of totality as the epitome of contradictions means that society is not merely riven and disturbed by contradictions and disproportionalities; rather, society becomes a totality only by virtue of its contradictions. The societalization of society, its consolidation into what—in vindication of Hegel—is truly more like a system than an organism, has resulted from the principle of domination, the principle of division itself, and it perpetuates it. Society has survived, reproduced, and extended itself, and has developed its forces, only through its division into the opposing interests of those who command and those who produce. Hegel maintained his awareness of this in the face of all sentimentality, all romanticism, all regressive return of thought and reality to past stages. Either the totality comes into its own by becoming reconciled, that is, it abolishes its contradictory quality by enduring its contradictions to the end, and ceases to be a totality; or what is old and false will continue on until the catastrophe occurs. As something contradictory, society as a whole moves beyond itself. The Goethean-Mephistophelian principle that everything that comes into being deserves to perish means in Hegel that the destruction of each individual thing is determined by individualization itself, by particularity, the law of the whole: "The individual by itself does not correspond to its concept. It is this limitation of its existence which constitutes the finitude and the ruin of the individual."[28] As something split off and detached, the individual is in the wrong when regarded from the point of view of justice and a peace that would be free of the pressure of the whole. By attending only to their own advantage, individuals are delivered over to limitation, stupidity, and insignificance; a society that is held together and survives only through the universal moment in the particular advantage fails completely as a consequence of its driving force: these formulations are not metaphorical dialectical ways of expressing simple statements about factual matters, not merely a flirtation with Hegel, as Marx says later in a celebrated passage. Instead, in a certain sense they translate Hegelian philosophy back into what it had projected into the language of the absolute. As though the dialectic had become frightened of itself, in the *Philosophy of Right* Hegel broke off such thoughts by abruptly absolutizing one category—the state. This is due to the fact that while his experience did indeed ascertain the limits of bourgeois society, limits contained in its own tendencies, as a bourgeois idealist he stopped at that boundary because he saw no real historical force on the other side of it. He could not resolve the contradiction between his dialectic and his experience: it was this alone that forced Hegel the critic to maintain the affirmative.

The central nerve of the dialectic as a method is determinate negation. It is based on the experience of the impotence of a criticism that keeps to the general and polishes off the object being criticized by subsuming it from above under a concept as its representative. Only the critical idea that unleashes the force stored up in its own object is fruitful; fruitful both for the object, by helping it to come into its own, and against it, reminding it that it is not yet itself. Hegel felt the sterility of all so-called intellectual work that takes place within the general sphere without dirtying itself with the specific; but rather than lament it he gave it a critical and productive turn. The dialectic expresses the fact that philosophical knowledge is not at home in the place where tradition has settled it, a place where it flourishes all too easily, unsaturated, as it were, with the heaviness and the resistance of what exists. Philosophical knowledge begins only where it opens up things that traditional thought has considered opaque, impenetrable, and mere products of individuation. Hegel's dialectical statement, "The real is nothing but an identity of the general and the particular,"[29] refers to this. But this shift is not intended to reward philosophy for its effort by returning it to ascertaining the data of an incoherent existence, and ultimately to positivism. No doubt there is a secret positivist impulse at work in Hegel in his deification of the quintessence of what is. But the force that specific individual knowledge reveals is always that of the inadequacy of its mere individuality. What it is is always more than itself. To the extent to which the whole is at work in the microcosm of the individual, one has grounds for speaking about a reprise of Leibniz in Hegel, however decidedly Hegel opposes the abstractness of the monad in other respects. To explain that in terms of unreflected intellectual experience: if someone wants to gain knowledge of something rather than cover it up with categories, he will have to surrender to it without reservation, without the cover of preconceptions, but he will not succeed unless the potential for the knowledge that is actualized only through immersion in the object is already waiting in him as theory. To this extent the Hegelian dialectic follows, with philosophical self-consciousness, the path of all productive thought, that is, all thought that does not simply reconstruct or recapitulate what has come before. That path, to be sure, is concealed from it; one might almost believe, with Hegel, that it has to be hidden from it in order for thought to be productive. It is neither a theory arrived at by induction nor one from which one could make deductions. What most shocks the innocent reader of the *Phenomenology of Spirit*, the sudden flashes of illumination that link the highest speculative ideas with the actual political experience of the French Revolution and the age of Napoleon, is what is actually dialectical. It links the general concept and the aconceptual τόδε τι—as perhaps Aristotle did the πρώτη οὐσία—each in itself, to its opposite, a kind of permanent explosion ignited by the contact of extremes. The Hegelian concept of the dialectic acquires its specific character, and distinguishes itself from shallow versions in vitalist philosophy like that of Dilthey, through its movement in and through the extremes: development as discontinuity. But it too arises from the experience of an antagonistic society; it does not originate in some mere conceptual schema. The history of an unreconciled epoch cannot be a history of harmonious development: it is only ideology, denying its antagonistic character, that makes it harmonious. Contradictions, which are its true and only ontology, are at the same time the formal law of a history that advances only through contradiction and with unspeakable suffering. Hegel referred to history as a "slaughterbench,"[30] and despite his much-cited optimism about history—Schopenhauer called it vile—the fiber of Hegel's philosophy, the consciousness that everything that exists both negates itself in coming into its own and perishes is by no means so different from Schopenhauer's *Ein Gedanke* as the official history of philosophy, repeating Schopenhauer's invectives, would have it.

Hegel's notion that it is only the idea that saturates itself with the weight of its object rather than shooting out beyond it without delay that, as "determinate negation," is worth anything, has, of course, entered the service of the apologetic aspect, the legitimation of what exists. The idea, which becomes truth only by completely absorbing what opposes it, repeatedly succumbs to the temptation to explain that what resists it is itself idea, truth. For that theory of Hegel's has recently been cited by Georg Lukács,[31] not only in order to defame literature that deviates from empirical reality, but above and beyond that to revive one of Hegel's most dubious theses, that of the rationality of the real.

According to Hegel's distinction between abstract and real possibility, only something that has become real is actually possible. This kind of philosophy sides with the big guns. It adopts the judgment of a reality that always destroys what could be different. Even, here, however, one should not judge Hegel solely on the basis of one's convictions. Persistent involvement with Hegel teaches one—and this is probably true of every great philosophy—that one cannot select what one likes from his philosophy and reject what one finds irritating. It is this grim necessity and not an ideal of completeness that makes Hegel's claim to system a serious and substantial one. The truth of that claim lies in the *skandalon,* not in its plausibility. Hence rescuing Hegel—and only rescue, not revival, is appropriate for him—means facing up to his philosophy where it is most painful and wresting truth from it where its untruth is obvious. Aesthetic experience may help us to do this with the doctrine of abstract and real possibility. Let me quote from a letter about Thomas Mann's late novella *The Black Swan* [*Die Betrogene*], from 1954:

If I am not mistaken, the figure of Ken has all the earmarks of an American from the late forties or the fifties and not from the decade following the First World War. . . . Now, one might say that this is a legitimate exercise of artistic freedom, and that the demand for chronological fidelity is secondary, even when it is a question of extreme precision in the portrayal of human beings. But I doubt whether this argument, which comes up as though it were self-evident, is truly valid. If you set a work in the 1920s and have it take place after the First rather than the Second World War, then you have good reasons for doing so—the most obvious being that someone like Frau von Tümmler is unimaginable today; at a deeper level the attempt to distance what is closest to hand is probably involved—to transpose it magically to a prehistoric world, the same world with whose special patina *Krull* is also concerned. But with this kind of transposition of the dates one assumes a kind of obligation, as in the first measure of a piece of music, whose desiderata remain with one until the last note, which achieves equilibrium. I do not mean the obligation of external fidelity to "period color" but rather that the images the work of art conjures up must manifest themselves as historical images at the same time, an obligation that for immanent aesthetic reasons can hardly dispense with that external obligation. For if I am not mistaken, one runs up against the paradoxical state of affairs that the evocation of such images, that is, that which is actually magical about the art object, is more successful, the more authentic the empirical details are. One would almost think that there is not a simple opposition between the permeation of the work with subjectivity and the demands of realism, which in a certain sense resound throughout the whole of your oeuvre, such as our education and history would lead us to think—but that instead the greater the precision one maintains with regard to the historical details, including those regarding types of human beings, the more likely one is to achieve spiritualization and attain the world of the *imago*. I first arrived at these eccentric thoughts by way of Proust, who in this regard reacted with idiosyncratic exactness, and they came to me again in reading the *Black Swan*. At the moment it seems to me as though this kind of precision can atone for some of the burden of sin under which every artistic fiction labors; it is as though that fiction could be healed of itself through exact imagination.[32]

Something similar lies behind Hegel's theorem. Even in the work of art, which is essentially different from all mere existing things by virtue of its own formal law, the fulfillment of this formal law, its own essential nature, its "possibility" in the emphatic sense, depends on the degree of reality it has absorbed into itself, no matter how transformed and reconfigured that reality may be. Even the idea that opposes reality in holding fast to a possibility that is repeatedly defeated does so only by regarding that possibility from the point of view of its realization, as a possibility for reality, something that reality itself, however weakly, is putting out feelers to, and not something that "would have been so nice," the tone of which resigns itself to failure from the outset. That is the truth content of Hegel's philosophy, even in those layers of it where, as in his philosophy of history and especially the preface to the *Philosophy of Right,* he resigns himself to reality or appears to vindicate it while sneering at those who would reform the world. It was the most reactionary and not at all the liberal progressive elements in Hegel that paved the way for a later socialist critique of abstract utopianism—only, of course, in the further history of socialism to provide in turn the pretext for a renewed repression. The defamation of all thought that protests the grim immediacy of what goes on in the Eastern zone under the name of praxis, a defamation that is customary there nowadays, is the most extreme evidence of this. But one should not hold Hegel responsible for the misuse of his motifs to drape a mantle of ideology over the ongoing horror. Dialectical truth lays itself open to such misuse: it is fragile by nature.

At the same time, there is no denying the untruth of Hegel's justification of what exists—something the Left-Hegelians rebelled against in their day and which in the meantime has increased to the point of absurdity. More than any other of his teachings, that of the rationality of the real seems to contradict the experience of reality, including that of its so-called overall tendency. But that idea is identical with Hegelian idealism. A philosophy for which all that exists dissolves into spirit as a result of its movement and as the totality of that movement, and which therefore proclaims the identity of subject and object in the whole when it is their nonidentity in the particular that inspires it— such a philosophy will apologetically take the side of what exists, which is supposed to be identical with spirit. But just as reality proved the thesis of the rationality of the real to be wrong, so the conception that characterizes the philosophy of identity has failed to hold up philosophically. The difference between subject and object cannot be eradicated in theory any more than it has been resolved in the experience of reality to the present. If the history of Hegelian philosophy after Hegel seems a weakening, a resignation of the power to comprehend and construct, when compared with the efforts of spirit, which were never more powerful than in Hegel's comprehension of the real, nevertheless, the process that brought it to that point is irreversible. It cannot be attributed solely to intellectual shortsightedness, forgetfulness, and an unfortunately reemergent naiveté. In good, and frightening, Hegelian fashion, the logic of the matter itself is at work in that process. The philosophical idea that what perishes merits its fate proves true, even for Hegel himself; as the ur-bourgeois thinker, Hegel is subject to Anaximander's ur-bourgeois maxim. Reason becomes incapable of comprehending reality not merely because of its own impotence but because reality is not reason. The debate between Kant and Hegel, in which Hegel's devastating argument had the last word, is not over; perhaps because what was decisive, the superior power of logical stringency, is untrue in the face of the Kantian discontinuities. Through his critique of Kant, Hegel achieved a magnificent extension of the practice of critical philosophy beyond the formal sphere; at the same time, in doing so he evaded the supreme critical moment, the critique of totality, of something infinite and conclusively given. Then he highhandedly did away with the barrier after all, with the experience of something that cannot be dissolved in consciousness, which was the innermost experience of Kant's transcendental philosophy, and he stipulated a unanimity of knowledge that becomes seamless through its discontinuities and that has something of a mythical illusory quality to it. Hegel thought away the difference between the conditioned and the absolute and endowed the conditioned with the semblance of the unconditioned. In the last analysis, by doing so he did an injustice to the experience on which he drew. The cognitive power of his philosophy vanishes along with its grounding in experience. The claim that he discloses the particular along with the whole becomes illegitimate, because that whole itself is not, as the famous sentence from the *Phenomenology* would have it, the true, and because the affirmative and self-assured reference to that whole as though one had a firm grasp of it is fictitious.

There is no way to make this criticism less harsh, but even so, it should not deal summarily with Hegel. Even where Hegel flies in the face of experience, including the experience that motivates his own philosophy, experience speaks from him. If the subject-object toward which his philosophy develops is not a system of reconciled absolute spirit, spirit nevertheless experiences the world as a system. The word "system," being more irrational than the word "life," captures the remorseless consolidation of all partial moments and acts of civil society into a whole through the principle of exchange more accurately, even if "life" is more appropriate to the irrationality of the world, its lack of reconciliation with the rational interests of a self-conscious humanity. But the rationality of that consolidation into a totality is itself irrationality, the totality of the negative. "The whole is the untrue," not merely because the thesis of totality is itself untruth, being the principle of domination inflated to the absolute; the idea of a positivity that can master everything that opposes it through the superior power of a comprehending spirit is the mirror image of the experience of the superior coercive force inherent in everything that exists by virtue of its consolidation under domination. This is the truth in Hegel's untruth. The force of the whole, which it mobilizes, is not a mere fantasy on the part of spirit; it is the force of the real web of illusion in which all individual existence remains trapped. By specifying, in opposition to Hegel, the negativity of the whole, philosophy satisfies, for the last time, the postulate of determinate negation, which is a positing. The ray of light that reveals the whole to be untrue in all its moments in none other than utopia, the utopia of the whole truth, which is still to be realized.

Skoteinos, or How to Read Hegel

Ich habe nichts als Rauschen.
I have nothing but murmuring.
Rudolf Borchardt

The ways in which Hegel's great systematic works, especially the
Science of Logic, resist understanding are qualitatively different
from those of other infamous texts. With Hegel the task is not
simply to ascertain, through intellectual effort and careful examination of the wording, a meaning of whose existence one has
no doubt. Rather, at many points the meaning itself is uncertain,
and no hermeneutic art has yet established it indisputably; and
in any case there is no Hegel philology and no adequate textual
criticism. For all their pettiness and *ressentiment,* Schopenhauer's
tirades about Hegel's alleged bombast evidenced a relationship
to the matter itself, at least negatively, like the child and the em-
peror's new clothes, in a situation where respect for culture and
fear of embarrassment merely dodge the issue. In the realm of
great philosophy Hegel is no doubt the only one with whom at
times one literally does not know and cannot conclusively determine what is being talked about, and with whom there is no
guarantee that such a judgment is even possible. One example

of this in matters of principle is the distinction between the categories of ground and causality in the second book of the *Logic;* a detailed example is provided by some sentences from the first chapter of that book:

Consequently, becoming is essence, its reflective movement, is the movement of nothing to nothing; and so back to itself. The transition, or becoming, sublates itself in its passage; the other that in this transition comes to be, is not the non-being of a being, but the nothingness of a nothing, and this, to be the negation of a nothing, constitutes being. Being only *is* as the movement of nothing to nothing, and as such it is essence; and the latter does not *have* this movement *within* it, but is this movement as a being that is itself absolutely illusory, pure negativity, outside of which there is nothing for it to negate but which negates only its own negative, which latter *is* only in this negating.[1]

There are analogous things in the early Hegel, even in his *Difference between Fichte's and Schelling's System of Philosophy,* the *Differenzschrift,* which is extremely clear as a prospectus. The conclusion of the section on the relationship of speculation to common sense reads,

The only aspect of speculation visible to common sense is its nullifying activity; and even this nullification is not visible in its entire scope. If common sense could grasp this scope, it would not believe speculation to be its enemy. For in its highest synthesis of the conscious and the non-conscious, speculation also demands the nullification of consciousness itself. Reason thus drowns itself and its knowledge and its reflection of the absolute identity, in its own abyss: and in this night of mere reflection and of the calculating intellect, in this night which is the noonday of life, common sense and speculation can meet one another.[2]

Only the ingenious and precise imagination of an impassioned member of a philosophical seminar will be able to illuminate the meaning of the last sentence, which is a match for Hölderlin's most advanced prose of the same years, without doing violence to it: that the "night of mere reflection" is night for mere reflection, but life, which is connected with noon, is speculation. For in Hegel the concept of speculation, removed from its terminological shell, means in turn none other than life forced to turn inward;[3] in this, speculative philosophy, Schopenhauer's included, and music are intimately related. The passage becomes susceptible of interpretation in the light of knowledge of the general train of Hegel's thought, especially the conceptual structure of the chapter, but it cannot be interpreted from the wording of the paragraph alone. To the person who holds doggedly to the wording and then in disappointment refuses to get involved with Hegel because of his unfathomable quality, one can offer little but generalities, with the inadequacy of which Hegel reproached the merely reflective understanding, as he calls it, in that text. One cannot simply skip over the passages in which it remains unclear what is being dealt with; their structure must be inferred from the substance of Hegel's philosophy. There is a sort of suspended quality associated with his philosophy, in accordance with the idea that truth cannot be grasped in any individual thesis or any delimited positive statement. Form in Hegel follows this intention. Nothing can be understood in isolation, everything is to be understood only in the context of the whole, with the awkward qualification that the whole in turn lives only in the individual moments. In actuality, however, this kind of doubleness of the dialectic eludes literary presentation, which is of necessity finite when it unequivocally states something unequivocal. This is why one has to make so many allowances for it in Hegel. That it cannot in principle achieve the unity of the whole and its parts at one blow becomes its weak spot. Every single sentence in Hegel's philosophy proves itself unsuitable for that philosophy, and the form expresses this in its inability to grasp any content with complete adequacy. If this were not the case, the form would be free of the poverty and the fallibility of concepts that Hegel tells us about. This is why understanding of Hegel decomposes into moments that are mediated by one another and yet contradictory. Hegel makes himself inaccessible to anyone who is not familiar with his overall intention. That intention is to be gleaned first and foremost from his critique of earlier philosophies and from his critique of his own times. At every point one must bear in mind, however provisionally, what Hegel is after; one must illuminate him from behind, so to speak. Hegel requires repeated readings, and requires them objectively and not merely to familiarize oneself with his subject matter. But if one stakes everything on this one can falsify him again. One then easily creates what has thus far been most injurious to interpretation, namely an empty consciousness of the system that is incompatible with the fact that the system is not intended to form an abstract higher-order concept with regard to its moments but rather to achieve its truth only in and through the concrete moments.

An essential element in Hegel himself lures one into this impoverished understanding from above. What is supposed to be the whole and the outcome of the whole—the construction of the subject-object, the demonstration that truth is essentially subject—is in fact presupposed by every dialectical step, in accordance with Hegel's own idea that the categories of being are already in themselves what his philosophy of the concept ultimately reveals their nature to be in and for itself. This is expressed most openly in Hegel's great *Encyclopedia of the Philosophical Sciences:*

This finitude of the End consists in the circumstance, that, in the process of realizing it, the material, which is employed as a means, is only externally subsumed under it and made conformable to it. But, as a matter of fact, the object is the concept implicitly: and thus when the

concept, in the shape of End, is realised in the object, we have but the
manifestation of the inner nature of the object itself. Objectivity is thus,
as it were, only a covering under which the concept lies concealed. Within
the range of the finite we can never see or experience that the End has
been really secured. The consummation of the infinite End, therefore,
consists merely in removing the illusion which makes it seem yet unac-
complished. The Good, the absolutely Good, is eternally accomplishing
itself in the world: and the result is that it needs not wait upon us, but
is already by implication, as well as in full actuality, accomplished. This
is the illusion under which we live. It alone supplies at the same time
the actualizing force on which the interest in the world reposes. In the
course of its process the Idea creates that illusion, by setting an antithesis to confront it; and its action consists in getting rid of the illusion
which it has created. Only out of this error does the truth arise. In this
fact lies the reconciliation with error and with finitude. Error or other-
being, when superseded, is still a necessary dynamic element of truth:
for truth can only be where it makes itself its own result.[4]

This gets in the way of that pure abandonment to the matter at
hand and its moments in which the introduction to the *Phenomenology* places its trust. Hegel does not operate so concretely as
that introduction would have it. The isolated moments go beyond themselves, in fact, only because the identity of subject and
object is preconceived. The relevance of the individual analyses
is repeatedly disrupted by the abstract primacy of the whole.
Most of the commentaries, however, McTaggart's included, fail
because they rely on the whole.[5] The intention is taken for the
deed, and orientation to the general direction of the ideas is taken
for their correctness; to follow them through would then be su-
perfluous. Hegel himself is by no means innocent of this inadequate way of proceeding. It follows the line of least resistance; it
is always easier to find one's bearings in an idea as on a map than
to examine the cogency of its elaboration. Thus Hegel himself
sometimes falters and makes do with formal declarations, theses
that say that something is so when the work has not yet been

done. Among the interpretive tasks whose time is ripe not the least and not the simplest is the separation of such passages from those in which thinking is really going on. Certainly in comparison with Kant the schematic elements are less prominent in Hegel. But the system often forcefully interferes with the program of "simply looking on" [*reines Zusehen*]. That was unavoidable if the whole were not to become hopelessly tangled. In order to prevent that, Hegel sometimes engages in pedantry, something that ill becomes one who has contemptuous things to say about verbal definitions and their like. Regarding the transition from civil society to the state, we read in the *Philosophy of Right,*

> The concept of this Idea has being only as mind, as something knowing itself and actual, because it is the objectification of itself, the movement running through the form of its moments. It is therefore (A) ethical mind in its natural or immediate phase—the Family. This substantiality loses its unity, passes over into division, and into the phase of relation, i.e. into (B) Civil Society—an association of members as self-subsistent individuals in a universality which, because of their self-subsistence, is only abstract. Their association is brought about by their needs, by the legal system—the means to security of person and property—and by an external organization for attaining their particular and common interests. This external state (C) is brought back to and welded into unity in the *Constitution of the State* which is the end and actuality of both the substantial universal order and the public life devoted thereto.[6]

In terms of content, the configuration of the dynamic-dialectical and the conservative-affirmative moments is as much a determinant of the excess of rigid generality in everything particular that comes into being as it is determined by it, and not only in the *Philosophy of Right*. Hegel's logic is not only his metaphysics; it is also his politics. The art of reading him should take note of where something new begins, some content, and where a machine that was not intended to be a machine is simply running and ought not to keep on doing so. At every moment one needs to keep two seemingly incompatible maxims in mind: painstaking immersion in detail, and free detachment. There is no lack of help available. What common sense would consider madness has its moments of clarity in Hegel, even for common sense. Common sense can use them to approach Hegel if it does not forbid itself to do so out of hatred—hatred being, of course, something Hegel himself, in the *Differenzschrift,* diagnosed as inherent in common sense.[7] Even the cryptic chapters have sentences like those in the discussion of illusory being [*Schein*] which express, after the fact, that subjective idealism and phenomenalism are intended polemically: "Thus *illusory being* is the phenomenon of scepticism, and the Appearance of idealism, too, is such an *immediacy,* which is not a something or a thing, in general, not an indifferent being that would still be, apart from its determinateness and connexion with the subject."[8]

The person who retreats to Hegel's overall conception when faced with Hegel's elaboration of his thoughts, substituting a determination of the position of the detail within the system for transparency in the individual analysis, has already renounced rigorous understanding, has capitulated because Hegel simply cannot be understood rigorously. Where Hegel is emphatically rejected—in positivism in particular—he is hardly even given consideration nowadays. Instead of being subjected to criticism, he is rejected as devoid of meaning. *Sinnleere,* or absense of meaning, is a more elegant word for the old accusation of insufficient clarity. Someone who cannot state what he means without ambiguity is not worth wasting time on. Like the desire for explicit definitions, to which it is related, this concept of clarity has survived the philosophy in which it originated and has become autonomous. The concept of clarity is taken from individual disciplines in which it has been preserved as dogma and reapplied to a philosophy that long ago subjected it to critical reflection and therefore ought not to have to comply with it unquestioningly. The Cartesian concepts of clarity and distinctness, still coupled with one another as late as Kant, are treated in the greatest detail in Descartes's *Principles of Philosophy:*

Indeed, in their whole lives, many men never perceive anything whatever accurately enough to make a sure judgment about it; because a perception upon which a sure and unquestionable judgment can rest must not only be clear, it must also be distinct. I call 'clear' that perception which is present and manifest to an attentive mind: just as we say that we clearly see those things which are present to our intent eye and act upon it sufficiently strongly and manifestly. On the other hand, I call 'distinct' that perception which, while clear, is so separated and delineated from all others that it contains absolutely nothing except what is clear.[9]

These sentences, which are of great consequence historically, are by no means as epistemologically unproblematic as sound common sense, now as then, might wish them to be. Descartes presents them as terminological stipulations: "claram voco illam . . . perceptionem." He defines clarity and distinctness for purposes of reaching agreement. Whether the knowledge itself, in its own character, satisfies the two criteria remains undetermined—for the sake of the method.* Cartesian doctrine does not bother with

---

*A philosophical history of clarity would need to reflect on the fact that originally clarity was both an attribute of the divine when contemplated and its mode of manifestation, the radiant aura of Christian and Jewish mysticism. With the ongoing process of secularization clarity becomes something methodological, a mode of knowledge made absolute—knowledge that satisfies its methodological rules, without regard to the derivation and aim of the ideal and without regard to the content. Clarity is the hypostatized form of accessible subjective consciousness of some object. It becomes a fetish for consciousness. Its adequacy to its objects suppresses the objects themselves and ultimately transcendent meaning as well; at that point philosophy is to be only a "striving for ultimate clarity." The word *enlightenment* probably marks the height of this development. Its depoten-

the phenomenology of cognitive acts—as though those acts were
to be dealt with like mathematical axiomatics, without regard to
their own structure. But it is this mathematical ideal that determines the two methodological norms, with respect to content as
well. Descartes knows no other way to explain them than through
comparison with the sensory world: "sicut ea clare a nobis videri
dicimus, quae, ocolo intuenti praesentia, satis fortiter et aperte
illum movent" [just as we say that we clearly see those things
which are present to our intent eye and act upon it sufficiently
strongly and manifestly].[10] One should not assume that precisely
here, in the discussion of clarity, Descartes was making do with
a mere metaphor—"sicut"—that of necessity diverges from what
it is supposed to explain and is itself therefore anything but clear.
He must have derived the ideal of clarity from sense certainty,
to which the talk about the eye alludes. But as we know, in Descartes its substratum, the sensory-spatial world, the *res extensa,* is
identical with the object of geometry, completely devoid of dy-
namics. Dissatisfaction with this idea produced Leibniz's theory
of an infinitesimal continuum leading from representations that
are obscure and confused to representations that are clear, an
idea taken up by Kant in opposition to Descartes:

Clearness is not, as the logicians assert, the consciousness of a representation. A certain degree of consciousness, though it be insufficient for
recollection, must be met with even in many obscure representations,
since in the absence of all consciousness we should make no distinction
between different combinations of obscure representations, which yet

tiation is no doubt connected with the fact that memory of the prototype of
clarity, light, which the pathos of clarity continues to presuppose, has since died
out. As though looking back to the past, the *Jugendstil,* a paradoxical truce between romanticism and positivism, formulated the double nature of clarity; a
motto of Jacobsen's reads, "Light over the land! that is what we wanted." When
Husserl discusses "levels of clarity," he is involuntarily using a metaphor from
the temple precincts of the *Jugendstil,* the profane sacred sphere.

we are able to do in respect of the characters of many concepts, such as those of right or equity, or as when the musician in improvising strikes several keys at once. But a representation is clear, when the consciousness suffices for the *consciousness of the distinction* of this representation from others.

In other words, it is "distinct" in the Cartesian sense, without that guaranteeing its truth. Kant continues,

If it suffices for distinguishing, but not for consciousness of the distinction, the representation must still be entitled obscure. There are therefore infinitely many degrees of consciousness, down to its complete vanishing.[11]

Kant would not have thought of devaluing all these levels other than the ideal highest level, any more than Leibniz would have. that highest level, however, is seized upon as clarity by the scientific concept of knowledge, just as though it were a thing in itself that was available at any time and at will, and just as though it had not, in the era after Descartes, shown itself to be a hypostasis. Rationalist in the historical sense, the ideal of clarity demands that knowledge trim and shape its object a priori, as though the object had to be a static mathematical object. The norm of clarity holds only where it is presupposed that the object itself is such that the subject's gaze can pin it down like the figures of geometry. When that ideal is declared to be generally valid, an a priori decision is made about the object, and knowledge, understood in the simplest sense of the scholastic and Cartesian *adequatio,* is supposed to orient itself accordingly. Clarity can be demanded of all knowledge only when it has been determined that the objects under investigation are free of all dynamic qualities that would cause them to elude the gaze that tries to capture and hole them unambiguously. The desideratum of clarity becomes doubly problematic when consistent thought discovers that the object of its philosophizing not only runs right over the knower as though on some vehicle but is inherently in motion, thereby divesting itself of its last similarity with the Cartesian *res extensa,* matter extended in space. The correlate of this insight is that the subject too is not static like a camera on a tripod; rather, the subject itself also moves, by virtue of its relationship to the object that is inherently in motion—one of the central tenets of Hegel's *Phenomenology.* Faced with this, the simple demand for clarity and distinctness becomes obsolete. The traditional categories do not remain intact within the dialectic; the dialectic permeates each of them and alters its inherent complexion.

Despite this, the praxis of knowledge clings to the primitive distinction between what is clear and what is unclear, a criterion that would be suitable only for a static subject and a static object. It does so, no doubt, out of excessive zeal for the specialized activities of the individual disciplines, which establish their objects and their object domains without reflection and set dogmatic norms for the relationship of knowledge to its objects. Clarity and distinctness take as their model a fixed consciousness of things, and in fact, in an earlier discussion of the ideal of clarity, Descartes, in the spirit of his system, talks about the thing in a naive-realistic manner:

And as I observed that in the words I think, hence I am, there is nothing at all which gives me assurance of their truth beyond this, that I see very clearly that in order to think it is necessary to exist, I concluded that I might take, as a general rule, the principle, that all the things which we very clearly and distinctly conceive are true, only observing, however, that there is some difficulty in rightly determining the objects which we distinctly conceive.[12]

In the difficulty Descartes notes, that of correctly determining what it is that we conceive distinctly, there stirs a faint memory of the fact that in the cognitive acts of the subject the objects themselves do not simply accommodate to that demand. If they did, clarity and distinctness, which for Descartes are attributes of truth, could not present difficulties in turn. But once it is acknowledged that clarity and distinctness are not mere characteristics of what is given, and are not themselves given, one can no longer evaluate the worth of knowledge in terms of how clearly and unequivocally individual items of knowledge present themselves. When consciousness does not conceive them as pinned down and identified like things—photographable, as it were—it finds itself of necessity in conflict with the Cartesian ambition. Reified consciousness freezes objects into things in themselves so that they can be available to science and praxis as things for others. Of course one cannot grossly neglect the demand for clarity; philosophy should not succumb to confusion and destroy the very possibility of its existence. What we should take from this is the urgent demand that the expression fit the matter expressed precisely, even where the matter at hand for its part does not conform to the customary notion of what can be indicated clearly. Here too philosophy is faced with a paradox: to say clearly something that is unclear, that has no firm outline, that does not accommodate to reification; to say it in such a way, that is, that the moments that elude the eye's fixating gaze, or that are not accessible at all, are indicated with the utmost distinctness. This, however, is not a merely formal demand but rather a part of the very substance philosophy is after. This demand is paradoxical because language and the process of reification are interlocked. The very form of the copula, the "is," pursues the aim of pinpointing its object, an aim to which philosophy ought to provide a corrective; in this sense all philosophical language is a language in opposition to language, marked with the stigma of its own impossibility. The position that would postpone the fulfillment of this demand—the idea that the requirement of clarity does not hold immediately or for the isolated individual part but is achieved through the whole—does not go far enough. As a systematic philosopher Hegel may have hoped to do this, but he did not fully redeem the promise. In actuality, philosophy eludes that demand, but it does so in the form of determinate negation. It has to take up that cause even with regard to presentation; to say concretely what it cannot say, to try to explain the limits of clarity itself. Philosophy does better to state that it will disappoint the expectation that it will fulfill its intention completely in every moment, every concept, and every sentence, than, intimidated by the success of the individual disciplines, to borrow a norm from them in terms of which it must declare bankruptcy. Philosophy is concerned with something that has no place within a pregiven order of ideas and objects such as the naiveté of rationalism envisions, something that cannot simply use that order as its system of coordinates and be mapped onto it. In the norm of clarity, the old copy theory of realism has entrenched itself within the critique of knowledge, unconcerned with the latter's actual results. Only that realism allows one to believe that every object can be reflected without question or dispute. But philosophy has to reflect on material concreteness, definition, and fulfillment just as it has to reflect on language and its relationship to the matter at hand. To the extent to which philosophy makes an ongoing effort to break out of the reification of consciousness and its objects, it cannot comply with the rules of the game of reified consciousness without negating itself, even though in other respects it is not permitted simply to disregard those rules if it does not want to degenerate into empty words. Wittgenstein's maxim, "Whereof one cannot speak, thereof one must be silent,"[13] in which the extreme of positivism spills over into the gesture of reverent authoritarian authenticity, and which for that reason exerts a kind of intellectual mass suggestion, is utterly antiphilosophical. If philosophy can be defined at all, it is an effort to express things one cannot speak about, to help express the nonidentical despite the fact that expressing it identifies it at the same time. Hegel attempts to do this. Because it can never be said directly, because everything direct and unmediated is false—and therefore necessarily unclear in its expression—he tirelessly says it in mediated form. This is one reason why Hegel invokes totality, however problematic that concept may be. A philosophy that relinquishes this effort in the name of a temptingly mathematicized formal logic denies its own concept a priori—its intention—and a constitutive part of that intention is the impossibility that Wittgenstein and his followers have turned into a taboo of reason on philosophy, a taboo that virtually abolishes reason itself.

Rarely has anyone laid out a theory of philosophical clarity; instead, the concept of clarity has been used as though it were self-evident.* In Hegel clarity is never made thematic; at most, this occurs *e contrario,* when Hegel defends Heraclitus: "The obscurity of this philosophy, however, chiefly consists in there being profound speculative thought contained in it; the concept, the idea, is foreign to the understanding and cannot be grasped by it, though it may find mathematics quite simple." [14] In terms of its meaning, if not literally, the desideratum of clarity is treated

*Alfred North Whitehead probably came closest in his metaphysical speculations in *Adventures of Ideas* (New York, MacMillan, 1932). Clarity and distinctness, he says, can exist only if the "subject" is posited as being strictly identical with the "knower" and the "object" with the "known": "No topic has suffered more from this tendency of philosophers than their account of the object-subject structure of experience. In the first place, this structure has been identified with the bare relation of knower to known. This subject is the knower, the object is the known. Thus, with this interpretation, the object-subject relation is the known-knower relation. It then follows that the more clearly any instance of this relation stands out for discrimination, the more safely we must utilize it for the interpretation of the status of experience in the universe of things. Hence Descartes' appeal to clarity and distinctness" (p. 225).

in Husserl's *Ideas;* the concept of exactness in that text should be equated with the traditional concept of clarity. Husserl reserves it for mathematical or definite manifolds [15] and asks whether his own phenomenological method must or can be constituted as a "geometry of experiences": [16] "Have we here also to seek after a definite system of axioms and to erect deductive theories upon it?" [17] Husserl's answer goes beyond that method. He has realized that the possibility of deriving deductive theories from a definite system of axioms cannot be determined methodologically, but only on the basis of content. This touches on the so-called exactness of concept formation, which according to Husserl is a condition of deductive theory. It is

in no sense a matter of our arbitrary choice and of logical dexterity but in respect of the assumed axiomatic concepts, which must however be presentable in immediate intuition, presupposes exactness in the apprehended essence itself. But to what extent "exact" essences can be found in an essence-domain, and whether exact essences figure in the substructure of all essences apprehended in real intuition, and therefore also of all the components of the essence, these are matters that depend throughout on the peculiar nature of the domain. [18]

In the next paragraph Husserl distinguishes descriptive from exact sciences and says of the former,

The *vagueness* of the concepts, the circumstances that they have mobile spheres of application, is no defect attaching to them; for they are flatly indispensable to the sphere of knowledge they serve, or, as we may also say, they are within this sphere the only concepts justified. If it behoves us to bring to suitable conceptual expression the intuitable corporeal data in their intuitively given essential characters, we must indeed take them as we find them. And we do not find them otherwise than in flux, and typical essences can in such case be apprehended only in that essential intuition which can be immediately analysed. The most perfect geometry and its most perfect practical control cannot help the descriptive student of nature to express precisely (in exact geometrical concepts) that which in so plain, so understanding, and so entirely suitable a way he expresses in the words: notched, indented, lens-shaped, umbelliform, and the like—simply concepts which are essentially and not accidentally inexact, and are therefore also unmathematical.[19]

Accordingly, philosophical concepts, as mobile concepts, are distinguished from exact concepts by virtue of the nature of what they attempt to grasp. At the same time, this sets limits to Husserl's insight. It acquiesces in the distinction between the fixed and the mobile, a distinction derived from the philosophy of reflection, whereas Hegel's dialectic defines each as inherently mediated by the other. But while Husserl is in other respects happy to join in the chorus that censures Hegel for his critique of the law of contradiction, as a logician Husserl concedes something that is certainly true of Hegel himself, who tried far more vigorously than Husserl to construct concepts in such a way that the life of the thing itself would be manifested in them, rather than constructing them in accordance with the abstract epistemological ideal of clarity: "Wholly immersed in the subject alone, he seemed to develop it only out of itself and for its own sake, scarcely out of his own spirit for the sake of those listening; and yet it sprang from him alone, and an almost paternal care for clarity attenuated the rigid seriousness that might have repelled the acceptance of such troublesome thoughts."[20]

If the demand for clarity gets tangled up linguistically because language does not actually permit the words themselves clarity— even in this regard the ideal of clarity converges with the mathematical—at the same time, in linguistic terms clarity is dependent on the attitude of thought to objectivity insofar as only what is true can be said with complete clarity. Complete transparency of expression depends not only on the relationship between expression and the matter represented but also on the soundness of the judgment. If it is unfounded or represents a false conclusion, it will resist adequate formulation; if it does not fully grasp the matter at hand, it will be vague in relation to it. Language, which is not an index of truth, is nevertheless an index of falsehood. But if Hegel's verdict that no individual sentence can be philosophically true holds outside his own work, then each sentence should also be confronted with its linguistic inadequacy. In Hegelian terms one could say—granted, without regard to Hegel's own linguistic praxis—that the unclarity for which he never ceases to be reproached is not simply a weakness; it is also the force that drives him to correct the untruth of the particular, an untruth that acknowledges itself in the unclarity of the individual sentence.

Best able to meet the demands of this predicament would be a philosophical language that would strive for intelligibility without confusing it with clarity. As an expression of the thing itself, language is not fully reducible to communication with others. Nor, however—and Hegel knew this—is it simply independent of communication. Otherwise it would elude all critique, even in its relationship to the matter at hand, and would reduce that relationship to an arbitrary presumption. Language as expression of the thing itself and language as communication are interwoven. The ability to name the matter at hand is developed under the compulsion to communicate it, and that element of coercion is preserved in it; conversely, it could not communicate anything that it did not have as its own intention, undistracted by other considerations. This dialectic plays itself out within the medium of language itself; it is not merely a fall from grace on the part of an inhumane social zeal that watches to make sure that no one thinks anything that cannot be communicated. Even a linguistic approach of the utmost integrity cannot do away with the antagonism between what is in itself and what is for others. While in literature this antagonism may go on behind the backs of the texts, so to speak, philosophy is compelled to take it into account. This is made more difficult by the historical moment, in which communication dictated by the market—the replacement of linguistic theory by communication theory is symptomatic of this— weighs upon language to such an extent that language forcibly puts a stop to communication in order to resist the conformity of what positivism calls "ordinary language." Language would rather become unintelligible than disfigure the matter at hand through a communication that gets in the way of communicating it. But the linguistic efforts of the theoretician run up against a limit that they have to respect if they do not want to sabotage themselves as much through fidelity as through infidelity. The moment of universality in language, without which there would be no language, does irrevocable damage to the complete objective specificity of the particular thing it wants to define. The corrective to this lies in efforts to achieve intelligibility, however unrecognizable those efforts may be. This intelligibility is the opposite pole to pure linguistic objectivity. The truth of expression flourishes only in the tension between the two. This tension, however, is not the same thing as the vague and brutal commandment of clarity, which for the most part amounts to the injunction that one speak the way others do and refrain from anything that would be different and could only be said differently. The requirement of clarity imposes a futile demand on language, a demand it wants fulfilled continuously, here and now, immediately. It asks something language cannot grant in the immediacy of its words and sentences—something it can grant only, and fragmentarily at that, in their configuration. Better would be an approach that carefully avoided definitions as mere stipulations and modeled concepts as faithfully as possible on what they say in language, making them virtually names. If nothing else, the later, "material" phenomenology was preparation for that. The effort the linguistic sensorium has to make to achieve precision is far greater than the mechanical effort to capture ordained definitions: he who makes himself the slave of his own words makes things easier for himself by shoving the words in front of the thing itself, however much he flatters himself that he is making it harder. Nevertheless, that way of proceeding is inadequate. For the words in empirical languages are not pure names but always θέσει, positings, as well, products of subjective consciousness which to that extent also resemble definitions. He who disregards this delivers himself over to a second kind of relativity in tearing words away from the relativity of definition, a second relativity that is a residue of the arbitrariness of how we are to understand them. Philosophical language has no remedy for this but to take care to use those words, which would necessarily fail if they were used literally as names, in such a way that their arbitrariness is decreased through their position. The linguistic configuration and the gaze focused intensely on the individual word complement one another. Together they explode the layer of mediocre tacit agreement, the sticky layer between understanding and the matter at hand. The true linguistic method could be compared with the way the emigré learns language. Impatient and under pressure, he may not use the dictionary as much as read whatever he can get access to. By that means, numerous words will be revealed in context but will be long surrounded by an outer area of indeterminateness, permitting ridiculous confusions, until the words decipher themselves through the abundance of combinations in which they appear and do so better and more fully than would have been possible with the dictionary, where even the choice of synonyms is affected by the lexicographer's narrowness and lack of linguistic sophistication.

One not insignificant reason for the refractoriness of Hegel's texts is probably that Hegel, with his excessive confidence in the objective spirit, believed that he could avoid this kind of admixture of the alien, that he could say the unsayable in his ordinary manner of speech. Despite this, the elements assembled in his work—concepts, judgments, syllogisms—are not unintelligible. It is only that they point beyond themselves and even in terms of their own idea are no more capable of fulfillment in isolation than are the components of extraphilosophical language, which are not aware that this is true of them. From this point of view, the task of understanding philosophy, and especially Hegel's philosophy, would be that of understanding the things that would not hold up before the current norm of clarity: thinking what is meant even where not everything implied in it can be represented *clare et distincte*. Seen from the point of view of science and scholarship, there is a moment of irrationality in the makeup of philosophical rationality, and it is up to philosophy to absorb this moment without thereby signing itself over to irrationalism. The dialectical method as a whole is an attempt to cope with this demand by freeing thought from the spell of the instant and developing it in far-reaching conceptual structures. Philosophical experience cannot dispense with exemplary obviousness, with the "this is the way it is" within the horizon of ineradicable vagueness. It cannot stop there, but the person for whom such obviousness does not flash out in any way during the reading of this or that weighty passage in Hegel's *Logic,* the person who does not notice what has been captured there, even if it is not fully articulated, will understand no more than a person enraptured with the vagueness of philosophical feeling. Fanatic proponents of clarity would like to extinguish such sudden flashes of illumination. Philosophy is supposed to pay in cash, and on the spot; involvement in philosophy is evaluated by means of the balance sheet, on the model of an expenditure of labor that has to have its equivalent in wages. But philosophy is a protest against the principle of equivalence, and in that regard it is unbourgeois even as bourgeois philosophy. The person who demands a pay-off from it—"Why should I be interested in this?"—is cheating himself of its lifeblood, the rhythm of continuity and intermittency in intellectual experience.

The specificity of philosophy as a configuration of moments is qualitatively different from a lack of ambiguity in every particular moment, even within the configuration, because the configuration itself is more, and other, than the quintessence of its moments. Constellation is not system. Everything does not become resolved, everything does not come out even; rather, one moment sheds light on the other, and the figures that the individual moments form together are specific signs and a legible script. This is not yet articulated in Hegel, whose mode of presentation is characterized by a sovereignly indifferent attitude toward language; at any rate it has not penetrated into the chemism of his own linguistic form. In its all-too-simpleminded confidence in the totality, the latter lacks the sharpness derived from the critical self-awareness that, in combination with reflection on the necessary disproportion, could bring the dialectic into language. This is deadly, because Hegel's formulations, which neither can be nor are intended to be conclusive, nevertheless often sound as though they were. Hegel's language has the demeanor of the language of doctrine. What gives it that air is the preponderance of quasi-oral delivery over the written text. Vagueness, something that cannot be eliminated in dialectic, becomes a defect in Hegel because he did not include an antidote to it in his language, although in other respects, in the subject matter of his philosophy, with its emphasis on and ultimately celebration of all kinds of objectivity, he provided it liberally. He would have preferred to write in the traditional philosophical manner, without the difference between his and traditional theory being reflected in his language. The loyal interpreter of Hegel has to take account of this deficiency. It is up to him to do what Hegel failed to do: to produce as much conciseness of formulation as possible in order to reveal the rigor of the dialectical movement, a rigor that is not content with such conciseness. There is probably no one for whom the philological norm—problematic in any case—of teasing out the author's subjectively intended meaning is less appropriate than Hegel. For his method, which cannot be separated from the matter at hand, is intended to set its object in motion, not to develop his own thoughts. His texts are not fully worked out—which necessarily means individuated—because their intellectual medium is also not fully worked out in the way we have come to take for granted in the hundred and fifty years since then. At that time one provided key words for the reader, entrances, as it were, such as occur in music. In the *Science of Logic,* this kind of aprioristic communication then becomes the ferment of a noncommunicative text and makes it hermetic.

The most widespread objection to Hegel's alleged lack of clarity is that of equivocation; we find it even in Überweg's *History of Philosophy.*[21] Hegel's philosophy teems with examples of equivocation. At the beginning of the *Subjective Logic,* for instance:

What the nature of the concept is, can no more be stated offhand than can the concept of any other object. . . . Now although it is true that the concept is to be regarded, not merely as a subjective presupposition but as the absolute foundation, yet it can be so only in so far as it has made itself the foundation. Abstract immediacy is no doubt a first; yet in so far as it is abstract it is, on the contrary mediated, and therefore if it is to be grasped in its truth its foundation must first be sought. Hence this foundation, though indeed an immediate, must have made itself immediate through the sublation of mediation.[22]

Without question, the concept of the concept [*Begriff*] is used differently at the two different points. In one case emphatically, as "absolute foundation," that is, objectively, in the sense of the thing itself, which is essentially spirit; but concepts are to be not only that but also the "subjective presupposition," something made, under which thought subsumes its Other. The terminology is confusing because even in the second case it is the singular and not, as one would expect, the plural that is used, probably because in principle the idea that the concept is the result of subjective synthesis is as much a part of Hegel's concept of the concept as the idea that it expresses the inherent nature of the matter at hand. In contrast to many other Hegelian equivocations, the understanding of this one is made easier by the fact that the differences in the two concepts of the concept are made thematic in the chapter "The Concept in General." Hegel provides the justification for this equivocation a few pages later, when he expounds on the unity of the two concepts: "I will confine myself here to a remark which may help one to grasp the notions here developed and may make it easier to find one's bearings in them. The concept when it has developed into a concrete existence that is itself free, is none other than the I or pure self-consciousness."[23] The objective concept, which according to Hegel is the concept of the thing itself, which developed to become its existence, something existing in itself, is at the same time, according to the general thesis of Hegel's system, subjectivity. Hence in the last analysis the nominalistic side of the concept, as something subjectively formed, coincides with the realistic side, the concept as something existing in itself, which in the course of the mediations of the *Logic* is itself shown to be subject, ego. This structure is prototypical for the mediocre quality of the objections to Hegel's equivocations. Where Hegel is formally guilty of equivocation, it is usually a question of points he is making that are germane to the content, an explication of how two distinct moments are both different and one and the same. Objections that are transcendent to Hegel scarcely touch him. Such objections assume the principle of identity: terms must remain within the meaning once given them by definition. This is pure nominalism; concepts should be nothing but identification tags for the unifying characteristics of a manifold. The more subjective their formation, the less one should attack them, as if their external, artificial quality would thereby be revealed. Common sense rationalizes this by saying that violating the definition would destroy order in thinking. This protest seems so unamenable to challenge because it is based on a conception that does not want to know about anything in the object that could give the lie to what subjective spirit has imposed on it. That conception energetically resists the experience that wants to let the matter at hand speak for itself, perhaps suspecting that in the face of that experience its own seemingly incorruptible concept of truth would be led to confess its untruth. Nominalism is part of the bourgeois bedrock; it accompanies the consolidation of urbanism across all its phases, and in the most diverse nations the ambivalence of that process is sedimented in it. Nominalism helps to free consciousness from the pressure of the authority of the concept that had established itself as universality; it does so by disenchanting the concept and making it a mere abbreviation for the particularities it covers. But such enlightenment is always also its opposite: hypostasis of the particular. To this extent nominalism encourages the bourgeoisie to be suspicious of everything that would restrain isolated individuals in their "pursuit of happiness," the unreflective pursuit of their own advantage, as being mere illusion. Nothing universal should exist that would remove the blinders of the particular, the belief that its contingency is its law. "What's a concept anyway?"—this gesture always expresses something else as well: that the individual has money to earn and that is more important than anything else. If the concept were to be autonomous in such a way that it did not exhaust itself in the particulars of which it is composed, the bourgeois principle of individuation would be shaken to its core. But that principle is all the more spitefully defended for being illusion; all the more so in that universality in the bad sense realizes itself through individual interests and buries individual interests beneath it in turn. This illusion is stubbornly maintained because otherwise those who are under its spell could no longer continue on unchallenged, nor could they continue to believe in the metaphysics of "what's mine is mine," the sacredness of possession as such. From this point of view, individuality is the subject become property. Nominalism, which is anti-ideological, has been ideology from the very beginning. Hegel's *Logic* wanted to develop this dialectic with its own means, which are not obviously reflections of society—leaving an ideological residue, namely that for the liberal the universality that rules in and above individuals would be transfigured and would become something positive. Only this kind of ideological turn permits Hegel to neutralize the social dialectic of the general and the particular by making it a logical one. In being proclaimed reality, the concept, which for Hegel is to be reality, remains concept. But for Hegel, as for Plato, the measure of the concept is the claim made by the matter at hand and not the subject's definitory activity. Hence Hegel suspends the identity of the concept as a criterion of truth. It is only that criterion, however, that degrades to the status of equivocation something that changes the meaning of concepts for the sake of their own substance.

Still, Hegel did not simply overturn the principle of identity; rather, he restricted it, despising and respecting it at the same time in his way. Only by virtue of that principle, that is, only when the life of the thing expressed by the concept is compared with the meaning specified and when the old meaning is thereby dishonored as invalid, is the other meaning constituted. On the one hand, Hegel handles terms the way nonphilosophical language unthinkingly treats many of its words and word classes: as the occasion requires. While some layers of meaning remain constant in such words, others are acquired according to the context. Philosophical language is patterned on naive language to the extent that, skeptical of scientific language, it uses context to soften the rigidity of its system of definition. In Hegel such occasional equivocations occur with expressions like the *"unmittelbar"* [unmediated or immediate] he uses so lavishly. When Hegel wants to say that the mediation is in the thing itself and not between several things, he often uses *"unmittelbar"* for things that are mediated [*"mittelbar"*]: to say that a category is *unmittelbar* its opposite thus means something like, it is its opposite in itself, rather than only through relationship to something external to it. "The exclusive reflection is thus a positing of the positive as excluding its opposite, so that this positing is immediately the positing of its opposite which it excludes."[24] Accordingly, mediation is itself immediate, because what is posited, mediated, is nothing different from what is primary, because this itself is posited. Similarly, and even more blatantly, he says in a later note, "It is very important to notice that the unmediated identity of form is posited here without the movement of the fact itself, a movement pregnant with content. It occurs in the fact as this is in its beginning. Thus pure being is immediately nothing."[25] Here "immediately" sounds simply paradoxical, but what is meant is that nothing is not a category added to pure being from the outside; instead, as something utterly unspecified, pure being is in itself nothing. A thoroughgoing terminological analysis of Hegel's language could make a complete listing of such equivocations and presumably clarify them. It would have to deal with technical terms like *Reflexion* [reflection] as well. Following a distinction current in post-Kantian idealism, that word covers the finite, restricted use of the intellect and, somewhat more broadly, the positivistic scientific attitude as a whole; but it also covers, within the overall architecture of the *Logic,* the *"Reflexionsbestimmungen,"* the determinations of reflection, that is, the critical reflection of the objective, initial, quasi-Aristotelian theory of the categories, which is then convicted in turn of being illusory and is led onward to the emphatic concept of the concept.

On the other hand, the equivocations may really be equivocations: a philosophical technique through which the dialectic of thought hopes to realize itself in language, occasionally with a somewhat heavy-handed tendency, anticipating Heidegger, to give linguistic states of affairs autonomy vis-à-vis what is meant, less emphatically than in Heidegger, certainly, and therefore more innocently. In the *Phenomenology,* for instance, Hegel is already juggling the meaning of *"Erinnerung"* [recollection or inwardization]:

As its fulfillment consists in perfectly knowing what it is, in knowing its substance, this knowing is its withdrawal into itself in which it abandons its outer existence and gives its existential shape over to recollection. Thus absorbed in itself, it is sunk in the night of its self-consciousness; but in that night its vanished outer existence is preserved, and this transformed existence—the former one, but now reborn of the Spirit's knowledge—is the new existence, a new world and a new shape of Spirit. In the immediacy of this new existence the Spirit has to start afresh to bring itself to maturity as if, for it, all that preceded were lost and it had learned nothing from the experience of the earlier Spirits. But recollection, the inwardizing, of that experience, has preserved it and is the inner being, and in fact the higher form of the substance. So although this Spirit starts afresh and apparently from its own resources to bring itself to maturity, it is none of the less on a higher level that it starts.[26]

The most hackneyed functional equivocation is that with *"aufheben"* [cancel, preserve, sublate], but this technique can be observed in more subtle cases as well, secret plays on words; Hegel plays tricks with the concept of nothingness in particular. Such linguistic figures should be taken not literally but ironically, as foolery. Without batting an eye, Hegel uses language to convict language of the empty pretense of its self-satisfied meaning. The function of language in such passages is not apologetic but critical. It disavows the finite judgment that in its particularlity acts as though it had the absolute truth, objectively and without being able to do anything about it. Equivocation is intended to demonstrate, with logical means, the inappropriateness of static logic for something that is inherently mediated and that by virtue of existing is in the process of becoming. Turning logic against itself is the dialectical salt in such equivocations.

The current understanding of equivocation should not be accepted uncritically. A semantic analysis that dissects equivocations scientifically is a necessary but by no means sufficient condition of a linguistic stocktaking of philosophy. To be sure, one cannot understand philosophy without separating the meanings of the terms "immanent" and its correlative "transcendent": the logical meaning, which has to do with whether or not thought remains within the presuppositions of the theorem with which it is concerned; the epistemological meaning, which has to do with whether the idea proceeds from the immanence of consciousness, the so-called context of the given within the subject; and the metaphysical meaning, which has to do with whether knowledge remains within the boundaries of possible experience. The choice of the same word for the different γένη, or genera, however, is not accidental, even in the current terminology. Thus the epistemological and metaphysical meanings of "transcendent" are connected; that which is absolutely transcendent in epistemological terms, the Kantian thing-in-itself, that is, that which cannot be found within the stream of consciousness, would also be metaphysically transcendent. Hegel extended that to the thesis that logic and metaphysics are one and the same. Even in predialectical logic, equivocations do not gloss over absolute differences but rather bear witness to the unity of what is different. Illuminating them requires insight into that unity as much as it requires noting the differences. Dialectical philosophy merely helped to self-consciousness a state of affairs that prevailed in traditional terminology and its history against its will. Hegel's equivocations feed on this state of affairs, even if in his thought the moment of distinction occasionally languishes in favor of the moment of undifferentiated sameness.

Such laxities notwithstanding, we find superlatives applied to language throughout Hegel's writings. Language is said to be the "perfect expression . . . for the mind,"[27] the "highest power possessed by mankind."[28] Nor does the *Logic* deviate from this. It deals with the "element of communication": "In the material world water fulfills the function of this medium; in the spiritual world, so far as the analogue of such a relation has a place there, the sign in general, and more precisely language, is to be regarded as fulfilling that function."[29] The *Phenomenology*, according to which language belongs to the stage of culture, tends in the same direction: "In speech, self-consciousness, qua independent separate individuality, comes as such into existence, so that it exists for others."[30] Accordingly it appears that Hegel, remarkably enough, did not admit language, which he accorded a place in the third book of the *Logic*, to the sphere of objective spirit but essentially conceived it as a "medium," or something "for others," as the bearer of contents of subjective consciousness rather than an expression of the Idea. Nominalistic features are nowhere absent in Hegel's system, which protests the customary dichotomy and considers itself compelled to absorb what is contrary to it, and whose tenor resists the futile effort to simply rescind the critique of the autonomy of the concept. To the extent to which he devoted his attention to it—and for a contemporary of Humboldt it is striking how little he concerned himself with language—Hegel wanted to see language more as what we would now think of as a means of communication than as the manifestation of truth that, strictly speaking, language, like art, ought to have been for him. His aversion to ornate and emphatic formulations is in harmony with this; he has unkind things to say about the "witty talk" of the spirit alienated from itself, of mere culture.[31] Germans had long reacted this way to Voltaire and Diderot. There lurks in Hegel the academic resentment of a linguistic self-reflection that would distance itself all too much from mediocre complicity; his stylistic indifference evokes his deadly readiness to make common cause with precritical consciousness through the reflection of reflection, to fortify the naive in their complaisance through unnaiveté. Hegel would hardly have wished for language to oppose that complicity, perhaps because his own linguistic experience, or deficiency, is precipitated in it. His linguistic praxis follows a slightly archaic conception of the primacy of the spoken over the written word, the kind of notion held by those who cling stubbornly to their dialect. The often-repeated remark, originally Horkheimer's, that only someone who knows Swabian can really understand Hegel, is no mere aperçu about linguistic idiosyncrasies; it describes the very gesture of Hegel's language. Hegel did not stop at scorn for linguistic expression, did not write professorially, unconcerned with expression—that practice did not become established until the era of the decline of the universities; instead, even if unconsciously, he raised his skeptical relationship to language, which inclined to lack of cogency, to a stylistic principle. He was forced into this by an aporia. He distrusted high-handed, in some sense brutal, linguistic expression and yet was forced to a specific linguistic form by the speculative nature of his philosophy, which was thoroughly detached from the common sense of everyday language. In its inconspicuous way, his solution was quite radical. As one who despised fully articulated language, he did not entrust himself to the language of culture, the current philosophical jargon, as something pregiven and mechanical, but instead, paradoxically, he challenged the principle of fixedness, which is indispensable for the existence of anything linguistic. Today we speak of antimatter; Hegel's texts are antitexts. While the extreme abstraction achieved and required by the greatest of his texts involves extreme efforts on the part of an objectivating thought that is detached from the immediacy of the experiencing subject, his books are not actually books but rather annotated lectures; often they are mere reverberations, not intended to be cogent even in published form. Eccentricities such as the fact that he edited only a small portion of his work, that most if it, even the full form of his complete system, exists only in the notebooks of his listeners or as a sort of manuscript draft that can be fully concretized only on the basis of the notes—these features are inherent in his philosophy. Throughout his life Hegel was an Aristotelian in wanting to reduce all phenomena to their form. This is how he proceeded even with the contingent phenomenon of the academic lecture. His texts are its Platonic idea. That a thought that made such extravagant claims should have foregone transmission in specific, definitive form can be explained only in terms of its ideal of presentation, the negation of presentation. At the same time, in the looseness of a delivery that even when most highly elaborated is closer to speech than to writing, one can look for a corrective to the hubris of the conclusive and definitive of which Hegel's work was accused even during his lifetime. By no means does this demeanor characterize only those parts of Hegel's system that exist merely as aids to memory and that he did not publish or published only in condensed form; on the contrary, it clearly becomes more extreme over the years. If pressed, one may regard the *Phenomenology* as a book; with the *Science of Logic* this is no longer possible. Reading the *Logic* calls to mind H. G. Hotho's description of the *Dozent* Hegel during his Berlin period:

Exhausted, morose, he sat there as if collapsed into himself, his head bent down, and while speaking kept turning pages and searching in his long folio notebooks, forward and backward, high and low. His constant clearing of his throat and coughing interrupted any flow of speech. Every sentence stood alone and came out with effort, cut in pieces and jumbled. Every word, every syllable detached itself only reluctantly to receive a strangely thorough emphasis from the metallic-empty voice with its broad Swabian dialect, as if each were the most important. . . . Eloquence that flows along smoothly presupposes that the speaker is finished with the subject inside and out and has it by heart, and formal skill has the ability to glide on garrulously and most graciously in what is half-baked and superficial. This man, however, had to raise up the most powerful thoughts from the deepest ground of things, and if they were to have a living effect then, although they had been pondered and worked over years before and ever again, they had to regenerate themselves in him in an ever living present.[32]

Hegel the lecturer rebelled against the hardened immanence of language, and in the process his own language ran into a brick wall. The first chapter of the first book of the *Logic* is a memorial to this intention, "Being, pure Being, without any further determination,"[33] an anacoluthon that tries with Hebelian cunning to find a way out of the predicament that "indeterminate immediacy," even if clothed in the form of a predicative statement like "Being is the most general concept, without any further determination," would thereby receive a definition through which the sentence would contradict itself. If one opposed this trick, saying that, strictly speaking, pure names cannot be understood and certainly cannot involve their contradictions, since only propositions, not mere concepts, contradict themselves, Hegel might shrewdly agree, noting that the objection motivates the first antithesis to his first thesis, and that he himself explains that such being is nothing. But in such sophistries a philosophy of identity that wants to have the last word even in the first, and at any price including the shabbiest, is not merely playing dumb. The dialectic's protest against language cannot be voiced directly except in language. Hence that protest is condemned to impotent paradox, and it makes a virtue out of that necessity.

The insights in Hotho's description go right to the core of Hegel's literary form. That form is the complete opposite of Nietzsche's maxim that one can only write about what one is finished with, what is behind one. The substance of Hegel's philosophy is process, and it wants to express itself as process, in permanent *status nascendi*, the negation of presentation as something congealed, something that would correspond to what was presented only if the latter were itself something congealed. To make an anachronistic comparison, Hegel's publications are more like films of thought than texts. The untutored eye can never capture the details of a film the way it can those of a still image, and so it is with Hegel's writings. This is the locus of the forbidding quality in them, and it is precisely here that Hegel regresses behind his dialectical content. To be consistent, that content would require a presentation antithetical to it. The individual moments would need to be so sharply distinguished linguistically, so responsibly expressed, that the subjective process of thought and its arbitrary quality would drop away from them. If on the contrary the presentation is assimilated without resistance to the structure of the dialectical movement, the price that the speculative concept's critique of traditional logic has to pay to the latter is set too low. Hegel did not deal with this adequately. A lack of sensitivity to the linguistic stratum as a whole may be responsible for this; the crudeness of some things in his aesthetics arouses that suspicion. Perhaps, however, the antilinguistic impulse in his thought, which perceives the limits of any particular existing thing as limits of language, was so deep that as a stylist Hegel sacrificed the primacy of objectification that governed his oeuvre as a whole. This man who reflected on all reflection did not reflect on language; he moved about in language with a carelessness that is incompatible with what he said. In the presentation his writings attempt a direct resemblance to the substance. Their significative character recedes in favor of a mimetic one, a kind of gestural or curvilinear writing strangely at odds with the solemn claims of reason that Hegel inherited from Kant and the Enlightenment. Dialects are analogous, like the Swabian with its untranslatable "Ha no," repositories of gestures that literary languages have given up. The romanticism that the mature Hegel treated with contempt, but which was the ferment of his own speculation, may have taken its revenge on him by taking over his language in its folksy tone. Abstractly flowing, Hegel's style, like Hölderlin's abstractions, takes on a musical quality that is absent from the sober style of the romantic Schelling. At times it makes itself felt in such things as the use of antithetical particles like "aber" [but] for purposes of mere connection:

Now because in the absolute, the form is only simple self-identity, the absolute does not determine itself; for determination is a form of difference which, in the first instance, counts as such. But because at the same time it contains all differences and form-determination whatever, or because it is itself the absolute form and reflection, the difference of the content must also appear in it. *But,* [emphasis added by Adorno] the absolute itself is absolute identity; this is its determination, for in it all manifoldness of the world-in-itself and the world of Appearance, or of inner and outer totality, is sublated.[34]

No doubt Hegel's style goes against customary philosophical understanding, yet in his weaknesses he paves the way for a different kind of understanding; one must read Hegel by describing along with him the curves of his intellectual movement, by playing his ideas with the speculative ear as though they were musical notes. Philosophy as a whole is allied with art in wanting to rescue, in the medium of the concept, the mimesis that the concept represses,[35] and here Hegel behaves like Alexander with the Gordian knot. He disempowers individual concepts, uses them as though they were the imageless images of what they mean. Hence the Goethean "residue of absurdity" in the philosophy of absolute spirit. What it wants to use to get beyond the concept always drives it back beneath the concept in the details. The only reader who does justice to Hegel is the one who does not denounce him for such indubitable weakness but instead perceives the impulse in that weakness: who understands why this or that must be incomprehensible and in fact thereby understands it.

Hegel has a twofold expectation of the reader, not ill suited to the nature of the dialectic. The reader is to float along, to let himself be borne by the current and not to force the momentary to linger. Otherwise he would change it, despite and through the greatest fidelity to it. On the other hand, the reader has to develop an intellectual slow-motion procedure, to slow down the tempo at the cloudy places in such a way that they do not evaporate and their motion can be seen. It is rare that the two modes of operation fall to the same act of reading. The act of reading has to separate into its polarities like the content itself. In a certain sense Marx's statement that philosophy passes over into history already characterizes Hegel.* With Hegel philosophy becomes

---

*"When reality is depicted, philosophy as an independent branch of knowledge loses its medium of existence. At the best its place can only be taken by a summing-up of the most general results, abstractions which arise from the observation of the historical development of men. Viewed apart from real history, these abstractions have in themselves no value whatsoever. They can only serve to facilitate the arrangement of historical material, to indicate the sequence of its

the activity of looking at and describing the movement of the concept, and in this sense the *Phenomenology of Spirit* outlines a virtual historiography of spirit. It is as though Hegel had hastily tried to model his presentation on this, to philosophize as though one were writing history, as though through one's mode of thinking one could force the unity of the systematic and the historical that is conceived in the dialectic. From this perspective the lack of *clarté* in Hegel's philosophy would be the result of the historical dimension intruding into it. The traces of the empirical element that is incommensurable with the concept take refuge in the presentation. Because that element cannot be fully permeated by the concept, it is inherently resistant to the norm of *clarté*, which, at first explicitly and later without remembering it, was derived from the ideal of a system that is opposed to historical reality as to all empirical reality. While Hegel is forced to integrate the historical moment into the logical, and vice versa, his attempt to do so turns into a critique of his own system. The system has to acknowledge the conceptual irreducibility of the concept, which is inherently historical: in terms of logical-systematic criteria the historical, all else notwithstanding, is disturbing; it is a blind spot. Hegel certainly saw that in the *Philosophy of Right,* although of course he thereby disavowed one of his central intentions and opted for the customary separation of the historical and the systematic:

To consider particular laws as they appear and develop in time is a purely historical task. Like acquaintance with what can be logically de-

separate strata" (Karl Marx, *The German Ideology,* in *The Marx-Engels Reader,* ed. Robert Tucker, New York: Norton, 1972, p. 119). A variant is even more pointed: "We know only a single science, the science of history. History can be regarded from two perspectives and can be divided into the history of nature and the history of mankind. The two cannot be separated; as long as human beings exist, the history of nature and the history of human beings determine one another" (*Marx-Engels Gesamtausgabe,* ed. D. Ryazonov, vol. 5, section 1, Berlin, Marx-Engels Archiv, 1932, p. 567).

duced from a comparison of these laws with previously existing legal principles, this task is appreciated and rewarded in its own sphere and has no relation whatever to the philosophical study of the subject—unless of course the derivation of particular laws from historical events is confused with their derivation from the concept, and the historical explanation and justification is stretched to become an absolutely valid justification. This difference, which is very important and should be firmly adhered to, is also very obvious. A particular law may be shown to be wholly grounded in and consistent with the circumstances and with existing legally established institutions, and yet it may be wrong and irrational in its essential character, like a number of provisions in Roman private law which followed quite logically from such institutions as Roman matrimony and Roman patria potestas. But even if particular laws are both right and reasonable, still it is one thing to prove that they have that character—which cannot be truly done except by means of the concept—and quite another to describe their appearance in history or the circumstances, contingencies, needs, and events which brought about their enactment. That kind of exposition and (pragmatic) knowledge, based on proximate or remote historical causes, is frequently called "explanation" or preferably "comprehension" by those who think that to expound history in this way is the only thing, or rather the essential thing, the only important thing, to be done in order to comprehend law or an established institution; whereas what is really essential, the concept of the thing, they have not discussed at all.[36]

In the conceptual aspect that resists the Hegelian movement of the concept, nonidentity gains the upper hand over the concept. Within that system, what would ultimately be the truth that would hold out against the system of identity becomes its blemish, that which cannot be represented. Hegel's readers have always been upset by this. Hegel, the restorationist liberal, is violating a bourgeois taboo. What is displayed is supposed to be finished, concluded, in accordance with the mores of the exchange of commodities, where the customer insists that what is delivered to him at full price should embody the full quantity of labor for which he is paying the equivalent. If there is anything left to be done on what he buys, he feels cheated. The conceptual labor and effort that Hegel's philosophy expects not merely of itself but also of the reader, in a sense that qualitatively surpasses every customary standard of reception, is held against him, as though he had not expended enough sweat. The taboo extends to the marketplace's idiosyncratic commandment that the traces of the human in the product be erased, that the product itself exist purely in itself. The fetish character of the commodity is not a mere veil; it is an imperative. Congealed labor in which one notices that the labor is that of human beings is warded off in disgust. Its human smell reveals its value to consist in a relationship between subjects rather than something adhering to objects, as it is perceived. Property, the category under which bourgeois society subsumes its spiritual goods as well, is not absolute possession. When that becomes evident, it seems as though what is most holy has been violated. Scholars are fond of becoming outraged about theorems and ideas they cannot take home fully proven. Discomfort with the conceptual character inherent in Hegel's philosophy is then rationalized to become the sneering assertion that the one incriminated cannot himself accomplish what he holds others to. Hence the well-known account of Hegel by Gustav Rümelin, the chancellor of Tübingen University. With unflaggingly cheap irony, Rümelin asks, "Do you understand it? Does the concept move around on its own in you, without any contribution from you? Does it change into its opposite, and does the higher unity of the contraries emerge from that?"[37] As though it were a question of the much-invoked—whether in admiration or derogation—"speculative mind" subjectively taking some special leaps in order to bring off something that Hegel ascribes to the concept itself; as though speculation were an esoteric capacity and not reflection's critical self-awareness, antagonistically and intimately related to reflection the way reason was related to the intellect in Kant. The first requirement for reading Hegel correctly is to rid oneself of deeply rooted habits like these, which the content of Hegel's philosophy shows to be false. It is useless to struggle and twitch like the caliph and the grand vizier in the form of storks, vainly pondering the word *mutabor*. The transformation of finite into infinite determinations that Hegel taught is neither a fact of subjective consciousness, nor does it require any special act. What is meant is a philosophical critique of philosophy, a critique just as rational as philosophy itself. The only subjective desideratum is not to become obstinate but rather to understand motivations, as with Kant and Fichte; nor does anyone capable of doing so need credulously to accept the movement of the concept as a reality sui generis.

These desiderata of a reading of Hegel, however, can be protected from divagation only if they are supplemented through the most acute and persistent attention to detail. Genetically, perhaps, the latter comes first; only when it fails categorically may the reader's dynamically detached attitude provide a corrective. What leads one to micrology is precisely the indisputable lack of differentiation between concepts and reflections: the lack of graphic power. At times even the legendary sympathetic reader of the early nineteenth century must feel his head spinning. The relationship of the categories to the whole is hardly ever emphatically distinguished from their specific restricted meaning in a specific passage. *"Idee"* [Idea] means on the one hand the absolute, the subject-object; but on the other hand, as the intellectual manifestation of the absolute it is supposed to be something other than the objective totality. Both appear in the *Subjective Logic*. There "Idea" often means the subject-object: "the absolute Idea alone is being, imperishable life, self-knowing truth, and is all truth,"[38] or: "the Idea has not merely the more general meaning of the true being, of the unity of concept and reality, but the more specific one of the unity of subjective concept and objectivity."[39] On the other hand, elsewhere in the same section of the *Subjective Logic,* the third, Hegel distinguishes the Idea from the objective totality:

Now the Idea has shown itself to be the concept liberated again into its subjectivity from the immediacy in which it is submerged in the object; to be the concept that distinguishes itself from its objectivity, which however is no less determined by it and possesses its substantiality only in that concept. . . . But this must be understood more precisely. The concept, having truly attained its reality, is the absolute judgement whose subject, as self-related negative unity, distinguishes itself from its objectivity and is the latter's being-in-and-for-self, but essentially relates itself to it through itself. . . .[40]

And correspondingly,

Now the determinateness of the Idea and the entire course followed by this determinateness has constituted the subject matter of the science of logic, from which course the absolute Idea itself has issued into an existence of its own; but the nature of this its existence has shown itself to be this, that determinateness does not have the shape of a content, but exists wholly as form, and that accordingly the Idea is the absolutely universal Idea.[41]

Finally he uses both in the same argument:

The Idea, namely, in positing itself as absolute unity of the pure concept and its reality and thus contracting itself into the immediacy of being, is the totality in this form—nature. But this determination has not issued from a process of becoming, nor is it a transition, as when above, the subjective concept in its totality becomes objectivity, and the subjective end becomes life. On the contrary, the pure Idea in which the determinateness or reality of the concept is itself raised into concept, is an absolute liberation for which there is no longer any immediate determination that is not equally posited and itself concept; in this freedom, therefore, no transition takes place; the simple being to which the Idea determines itself remains perfectly transparent to it and is the concept that, in its determination, abides with itself. The passage is therefore to be understood here rather in this manner, that the Idea freely releases itself in its absolute self-assurance and inner poise.[42]

Just as in Hegel "foul" existence is separated from the real that is rational, so despite everything the idea inevitably remains χωρις from reality, set apart from it, in that reality is also "foul" existence. Such incongruities are scattered throughout Hegel's most important texts. Hence the task is the disjunction of what is specific from what is more general, what is not due and payable *hic et nunc;* the two are intertwined in the linguistic figures Hegel likes to use. He was trying to ward off the danger of a flight into the general when he told a lady at a tea party who had asked him what one should be thinking at this or that point in his text, "precisely that." But the question was not as silly as the way it was dealt with makes it seem. The questioner may have noticed that empty consciousness, that is, what a paragraph accomplishes in terms of its logical coherence, usurps the place of actual accomplishment, whereas whether it requires that logic or not depends on what is accomplished. The question of what one should be thinking at any particular point voices a false demand insofar as it reports a mere lack of comprehension and hopes to be rescued through illustrations, which, as illustrations, miss the mark; but it quite properly means that every individual analysis has to be followed through, that in reading one must get hold of states of affairs that are discussed and accurately stated and undergo transformation, not mere guidelines. The most frequent weakness in interpretations of Hegel is that the analysis is not followed through in terms of the content; instead, the wording is merely paraphrased. For the most part such exegesis then bears the same relation to the thing itself as the road sign to the road one has traveled, as Scheler jokingly put it. In many cases Hegel himself did not carry out the activity of following through but replaced it with circumlocutious declarations of intention. In the *Philosophy of Right,* for instance, Hegel makes a pretense of a speculative deduction of monarchy but does not carry it out, and for that reason the results are vulnerable to all manner of criticism:

This ultimate self in which the will of the state is concentrated is, when thus taken in abstraction, a single self and therefore is immediate individuality. Hence its "natural" character is implied in its very conception. The monarch, therefore, is essentially characterized as this individual, in abstraction from all his other characteristics, and this individual is raised to the dignity of monarchy in an immediate, natural, fashion, i.e. through his birth in the course of nature. This transition of the concept of pure self-determination into the immediacy of being and so into the realm of nature is of a purely speculative character, and apprehension of it therefore belongs to logic. Moreover, this transition is on the whole the same as that familiar to us in the nature of willing, and there the process is to translate something from subjectivity (i.e. some purpose held before the mind) into existence (see Paragraph 8). But the proper form of the Idea and of the transition here under consideration is the immediate conversion of the pure self-determination of the will (i.e. of the simple concept itself) into a single and natural existent without the mediation of a particular content (like a purpose in the case of action). . . . Addition. It is often alleged against monarchy that it makes the welfare of the state dependent on chance, for it is urged, the monarch may be ill-educated, he may perhaps be unworthy of the highest position in the state, and it is senseless that such a state of affairs should exist because it is supposed to be rational. But all this rests on a presupposition which is nugatory, namely that everything depends on the monarch's particular character. In a completely organized state, it is only a question of the culminating point of formal decision . . .; he has only to say "yes" and dot the "i," because the throne should be such that the significant thing in its holder is not his particular make-up. . . . Whatever else the monarch may have in addition to this power of final decision is part and parcel of his private character and should be of no consequence. Of course there may be circumstances in which it is this private character alone which has prominence, but in that event the state is either not fully developed, or else is badly constructed. In a well-organized monarchy, the objective aspects belongs to law alone, and the monarch's part is merely to set to the law the subjective "I will."[43]

Either all the bad contingency that Hegel disputes is condensed into this "I will" after all, or the monarch is truly only a yea-sayer who could be dispensed with. Frequently, however such weaknesses also contain crucial aids to understanding. In better cases than the awkwardly ideological *Philosophy of Right,* immanent fidelity to Hegel's intention requires one to supplement or go beyond the text in order to understand it. Then it is useless to ponder cryptic individual formulations and get involved in often unresolvable controversies about what was meant. Rather, one must uncover Hegel's aim; the subject matter should be reconstructed from knowledge of it. He almost always has certain issues in mind even when his own formulations fail to capture them. What Hegel was talking about is more important than what he meant. The circumstances and the problem have to be developed from Hegel's program and then thought through on their own. In Hegel's philosophy the primacy of objectivity over the intended train of thought, the primacy of the specific state of affairs under consideration, constitutes an authority in opposition to his philosophy. If within a paragraph the problem at issue stands out as being outlined and resolved—and the secret of the philosophical method may lie in the fact that to understand a problem and to solve it are actually one and the same thing— then Hegel's intention becomes clear too, whether it is that the cryptic content of his thought now discloses itself of its own accord or that his thoughts become articulated through what they themselves missed.

The task of immersion in the detail requires consideration of the internal structure of Hegel's texts. It is not the customary progressive linear development of ideas, any more than it is a sequence of discrete, differentiated independent analyses. The comparison with a web that the structure sometimes provokes is also inaccurate: it ignores the dynamic moment. What is characteristic, however, is the fusion of the dynamic moment with the static. Hegel's weighty chapters resist the distinction between conceptual analysis, "commentary," and synthesis as progression to something new that is not contained within the concept itself. This makes it difficult to decide where to stop:

He faltered even in the beginning, tried to go on, started once more, stopped again, spoke and pondered; the right word seemed to be missing forever, but then it scored most surely; it seemed common and yet inimitably fitting, unusual and yet the only one that was right. . . . Now one had grasped the clear meaning of a sentence and hoped most ardently to progress. In vain. Instead of moving forward, the thought kept revolving around the same point with similar words. But if one's wearied attention wandered and strayed a few minutes before it suddenly returned with a start to the lecture, it found itself punished by having been torn entirely out of the context. For slowly and deliberately, making use of seemingly insignificant links, some full thought had limited itself to the point of one-sidedness, had split itself into distinctions and involved itself in contradictions whose victorious solution eventually found the strength to compel the reunification of the most recalcitrant elements. Thus always taking up again carefully what had gone before in order to develop out of it more profoundly in a different form what came later, more divisive and yet even richer in reconciliation, the most wonderful stream of thought twisted and pressed and struggled, now isolating something, now very comprehensively; occasionally hesitant, then by jerks sweeping along, it flowed forward irresistibly.[44]

Broadly speaking, one might say that in the Hegelian system, as in Hegel's oral delivery, analytic and synthetic judgments are not as strictly distinguished as in the Kantian ABC. In this regard as well, Hegel is composing something analogous to a musical reprise of pre-Kantian and especially Leibnizian rationalism, mediated by subjectivity, and this forms the pattern for his presentation. The presentation tends to take the form of the analytic judgment, little as Hegel liked that logical form, the abstract identity of the concept. The movement of thought, the entrance of something new, does not add anything to the grammatical concept that forms the subject, as it does with Kant. The new is the old. Through the explication of the concepts, in other words through what, according to traditional logic and epistemology, is accomplished by analytic judgments, the concept's Other, the nonidentical, becomes evident within the concept itself, something implied in its meaning, without the scope of the concept being infringed upon. The concept is turned this way and that until it becomes clear that it is more than what it is. The concept breaks up when it insists on its identity, and yet it is only the catastrophe of such tenacity that gives rise to the movement that makes it immanently other than itself. The model of this structure of thought is Hegel's treatment of the law of identity $A = A$, which is outlined in the *Differenzschrift* and then carried out energetically in the *Logic*. Inherent in the meaning of a pure identical judgment is the nonidentity of its members. In an individual judgment sameness can be predicated only of things that are not the same; otherwise the claim inherent in the form of the judgment—that something is this or that—is not met. Numerous reflections of Hegel's are organized in a similar manner, and one must have a clear grasp of this way of proceeding to avoid being repeatedly confused by it. In its microstructure Hegel's thought and its literary forms are what Walter Benjamin later called "dialectics at a standstill," comparable to the experience the eye has when looking through a microscope at a drop of water that begins to teem with life; except that what that stubborn, spellbinding gaze falls on is not firmly delineated as an object but frayed, as it were, at the edges. One of the most famous passages from the preface to the *Phenomenology* reveals something of that internal structure:

> Appearance is the arising and passing away that does not itself arise and pass away, but is 'in itself' . . . and constitutes the actuality and the movement of the life of truth. The True is thus the Bacchanalian revel in which no member is not drunk; yet because each member collapses as soon as he drops out, the revel is just as much transparent and simple repose. Judged in the court of this movement, the single shapes of Spirit do not persist any more than the determinate thoughts do, but they are as much positive and necessary moments, as they are negative and evanescent. In the whole of the movement, seen as a state of repose, what distinguishes itself therein, and gives itself particular existence, is preserved as something that recollects itself, whose existence is self-knowledge, and whose self-knowledge is just as immediately existence.[45]

Here, to be sure, and in analogous places in the *Logic*,[46] the standstill is reserved for the totality, as in Goethe's maxim about all striving being eternal rest. But like every aspect of the whole in Hegel, this one too is simultaneously an aspect of every individual part, and its ubiquity may have prevented Hegel from acknowledging it. He was too close to it; it concealed itself from him, a piece of unreflected immediacy.

But the internal structure also has far-reaching consequences for the way the whole fits together: it has retroactive force. The usual conception of the dynamic of Hegel's thought—that the movement of the concept is nothing but the advance from one to the other by virtue of the inner mediatedness of the former—is one-sided if nothing else. In that the reflection of each concept, which is linked with the reflection of reflection, breaks the concept open by demonstrating its inconsistency, the movement of the concept always also affects the stage from which it breaks away. The advance is a permanent critique of what has come before, and this kind of movement supplements the movement of advance by synthesis. In the dialectic of identity, then, not only is the identity of the nonidentical, as its higher form, the A = B, the synthetic judgment, attained; in addition, the content of the synthetic judgment is recognized as already a necessary moment of the analytic judgment A = A. Conversely, the simple formal identity of A = A is retained in the equivalence of the nonidentical. Often, accordingly, the presentation makes a backward leap. What would be new according to the simple schema of triplicity reveals itself to be the concept that formed the starting point for the particular dialectical movement under discussion, modified and under different illumination. The "self-determination of essence as ground" from the second book of the *Logic* provides evidence that Hegel himself intended this:

In so far as the determination of a first, an immediate, is the starting point of the advance to ground (through the nature of the determination itself which sublates itself or falls to the ground), ground is, in the first instance, determined by that first. But this determining is, on the one hand, as a sublating of the determining, only the restored, purified or manifested identity of essence which the reflected determination is in itself; on the other hand it is this negating movement as a determining that first posits that reflected determinateness which appeared as immediate, but which is posited only by the self-excluding reflection of ground and therein is posited as only a posited or sublated determination. Thus essence, in determining itself as ground, proceeds only from itself.[47]

In the *Subjective Logic* Hegel defines, in general terms and a little formalistically, the "third member" of the three-part schema as the first member, in modified form, of the individual dialectical movement under discussion:

In this turning point of the method, the course of cognition at the same time returns into itself. As self-sublating contradiction this negativity is the restoration of the first immediacy, of simple universality; for the other of the other, the negative of the negative, is immediately the positive, the identical, the universal. If one insists on counting, this second immediate is, in the course of the method as a whole, the third term to the first immediate and the mediated. It is also, however, the third term to the first formal negative and to absolute negativity or the second negative; now as the first negative is already the second term, the term reckoned as third can also be reckoned as fourth, and instead of a triplicity, the abstract form may be taken as a quadruplicity; in this way, the negative or the difference is counted as a duality. . . . Now more precisely the third is the immediate, but the immediate resulting from sublation of mediation, the simple resulting from sublation of difference, the positive resulting from sublation of the negative, the concept that has realized itself by means of its otherness and by the sublation of this reality has restored . . . its simple relation to itself. This result is therefore the truth. It is equally immediacy and mediation; but such forms of judgment as: the third is immediacy and mediation, or: it is the unity of them, are not capable of grasping it; for it is not a quiescent third, but precisely as the unity, is self-mediating movement and activity. . . . Now this result, as the whole that has withdrawn into and is identical with itself, has given itself the form of immediacy. Hence it is now itself the same thing as the starting-point had determined itself to be.[48]

Music of Beethoven's type, in which ideally the reprise, the return in reminiscence of complexes expounded earlier, should be the result of development, that is, of dialectic, offers an analogue to this that transcends mere analogy. Highly organized music too must be heard multidimensionally, forward and backward at the same time. Its temporal organizing principle requires this: time can be articulated only through distinctions between what is familiar and what is not yet familiar, between what already exists and what is new; the condition of moving forward is a retrogressive consciousness. One has to know a whole movement and be aware retrospectively at every moment of what has come before. The individual passages have to be grasped as consequences of what has come before, the meaning of a divergent repetition has to be evaluated, and reappearance has to be perceived not merely as architectonic correspondence but as something that has evolved with necessity. What may help both in understanding this analogy and in understanding the core of Hegel's thought is recognizing that the conception of totality as an identity immanently mediated by nonidentity is a law of artistic form transposed into the philosophical domain. The transposition is itself philosophically motivated. Absolute idealism had no more desire to tolerate something alien and external to its own law than did the dynamic teleology of the art of its time, classicistic music in particular. While the mature Hegel disparaged Schelling's "intellectual intuition" as an extravagant rapture that was simultaneously aconceptual and mechanical, in form Hegel's philosophy is incomparably closer to works of art than Schelling's, which wanted to construct the world using the work of art as its prototype. As something set off from empirical reality, art requires for its constitution something indissoluble, nonidentical; art becomes art only through its relation to something that is itself not art. This is perpetuated in the dualism of Schelling's philosophy, which derives its concept of truth from art, a dualism he never did away with. But if art is not an idea separate from philosophy and guiding it as a prototype, if philosophy as such wants to accomplish what is not accomplished in art, as illusion, then the philosophical totality thereby becomes aesthetic, an arena for the semblance of absolute identity. This semblance is less harmful in art insofar as art posits itself as semblance and not as actualized reason.

Just as there is a tension between expression and construction in works of art, so in Hegel there is a tension between the expressive and the argumentative elements. All philosophy that does not make do with an unreflective imitation of the scientific ideal is of course familiar with this tension in a less extreme form.

In Hegel the expressive element represents experience; that which actually wants to come out into the open but cannot, if it wants to attain necessity, appear except in the medium of concepts, which is fundamentally its opposite. This need for expression is by no means, and least of all in Hegel, a matter of subjective weltanschauung. Rather, it is itself objectively determined. It has to do, in all philosophy that is philosophy, with historically manifested truth. In the afterlife of philosophical works, the unfolding of their substance, what the works express is gradually extricated from what in them was merely thought. But the very objectivity of the experiential content which, as unconscious historiography of the spirit, overgrows what is subjectively intended, first stirs within philosophy, as though it were the subjective moment in it. Hence it gains strength from precisely the activity of thought that is ultimately extinguished in the experiential content that becomes evident. So-called foundational or ur-experiences that would attempt to express themselves directly as much, without subjecting themselves to reflection, would remain impotent impulses. Subjective experience is only the outer shell of philosophical experience, which develops beneath it and then throws it off. The whole of Hegel's philosophy is an effort to translate intellectual experience into concepts. The expansion of the apparatus of thought, often censured as being mechanical and coercive, is proportional to the force of the experience to be mastered. In the *Phenomenology* Hegel still wanted to believe that the experience could simply be described. But intellectual experience can be expressed only by being reflected in its mediation—that is, actively thought. There is no way to make the intellectual experience expressed and the medium of thought irrelevant to one another. What is false in Hegel's philosophy manifests itself precisely in the notion that with enough conceptual effort it could realize this kind of irrelevance. Hence the innumerable gaps between the concept and what is experienced. Hegel has to be read against the grain, and in such a way that every logical operation, however formal it seems to be, is reduced to its experiential core. The equivalent of such experience in the reader is the imagination. If the reader wanted merely to determine what a passage meant or to pursue the chimera of figuring out what the author wanted to say, the substance of which he wants to attain philosophical certainty would evaporate for him. No one can read any more out of Hegel than he puts in. The process of understanding is a progressive self-correcting of such projections through comparison with the text. The content itself contains, as a law of its form, the expectation of productive imagination on the part of the one reading. Whatever experience the reader may register has to be thought out on the basis of the reader's own experience. Understanding has to find a foothold in the gap between experience and concept. Where concepts become an autonomous apparatus—and only a foolish enthusiasm could claim that Hegel always respects his own canon—they need to be brought back into the intellectual experience that motivates them and be made vital, as they would like to be but are compulsively incapable of being. On the other hand, the primacy of intellectual experience in Hegel also affects the conceptual form. Hegel, who is accused of panlogism, anticipates a tendency that did not become explicit methodologically until the phenomenology of Husserl and his school a hundred years later. His intellectual mode of proceeding is paradoxical. While it remains, to an extreme degree, within the medium of the concept—at the highest level of abstraction in terms of the hierarchy of comprehensive logic—it does not actually argue as though it wanted thereby to economize on the objective contribution of thought as opposed to that of experience, which on the other hand is intellectual experience and even itself thought.

The program of pure onlooking outlined in the introduction to the *Phenomenology* carries more weight in Hegel's chief works than naive philosophical consciousness believes it to. Because as Hegel conceives it all phenomena—and for Hegel's *Logic* the categories of logic are also phenomena, things that are manifested, given, and in that sense mediated, something that had already been illuminated in a passage in Kant's deduction*—are inherently spiritually mediated, what is needed in order to grasp them is not thought but rather the relationship for which the phenomenology of a hundred years later invented the term "spontaneous receptivity." The thinking subject is to be released from thought, since thought will rediscover itself in the object thought; it has only to be developed out of the object and to identify itself in it. However subject to criticism this view may be, Hegel's mode of proceeding is organized in accordance with it. Hence he can be understood only when the individual analyses are read not as arguments but as descriptions of "implied meanings." Except that the latter are conceived not as fixed meanings, ideal unities, invariants, as in the school of Husserl, but rather as inherently in motion. Hegel distrusts argument deeply, and with good reason. Primarily because the dialectician knows something that Simmel later rediscovered: that anything that remains argumentation exposes itself to refutation. For this reason Hegel necessarily dis-

---

*"They are merely rules for an understanding whose whole power consists in thought, consists, that is, in the act whereby it brings the synthesis of a manifold, given to it from elsewhere in intuition, to the unity of apperception—a faculty, therefore, which by itself knows nothing whatsoever, but merely combines and arranges the material of knowledge, that is, the intuition, which must be given to it by the object. This peculiarity of our understanding, that it can produce a priori unity of apperception solely by means of the categories, and only by such and so many, is as little capable of further explanation as why we have just these and no other functions of judgment, or why space and time are the only forms of our possible intuition" (Kant, *Critique of Pure Reason*, trans. Norman Kemp Smith, London: MacMillan, 1963, p. 161 [B145f]).

appoints anyone who looks for his arguments. Even the question why, which the unarmed reader often feels himself obliged to ask of Hegel's transitions and deductions, where other possibilities than the one Hegel puts forth seem open, is inappropriate. The general orientation is set by the overall intention, but what is said about the phenomena is derived from the phenomena themselves, or is at least supposed to be. Categories like "foundational relations" themselves fall into the Hegelian dialectic of essence and should not be presupposed. The task Hegel imposes is not that of an intellectual forced march; it is almost the opposite. The ideal is nonargumentative thought. His philosophy, which, as a philosophy of identity stretched to the breaking point, demands the most extreme efforts on the part of thought, is also dialectical in that it moves within the medium of a thought freed from tension. Whether his philosophy is followed through to the end depends on whether this relaxation is attained or not. In this Hegel differs profoundly from Kant and Fichte; also, to be sure, from the intuitionism he attacked in Schelling. He broke up the dichotomy between thesis and argument as he did all rigid dichotomies. For him argument is not something subsidiary, as is often the case in philosophy, something that becomes dispensable as soon as the thesis has been firmly established. In his works there are neither theses nor arguments; Hegel made fun of theses, calling them "dicta." The one is, virtually, always the other as well: the argument is the predication of what something is, hence thesis; the thesis is synthesis through judgment, hence argument.

Relaxation of consciousness as an approach means not warding off associations but opening the understanding to them. Hegel can be read only associatively. At every point one must try to admit as many possibilities for what is meant, as many connections to something else, as may arise. A major part of the work

of the productive imagination consists in this. At least a portion
of the energy without which one can no more read than one can
without relaxation is used to shake off the automatic discipline
that is required for pure concentration on the object and that
thereby easily misses the object. For Hegel, associative thought
is grounded in the thing itself. Despite his declarations to the
contrary in the *Philosophy of Right,* both Hegel's conception of
the truth as something in the process of becoming and his ab-
sorption of empirical reality into the life of the concept transcended the division of philosophy into systematic philosophy
and historical philosophy. As we know, spirit, the substratum of
his philosophy, is not intended to be a separate, subjective idea;
it is intended to be real, and its movement to be real history.
Nevertheless, with incomparable tact, even the later chapters of
the *Phenomenology* refrain from brutally compacting the science
of the experience of consciousness and that of human history
into one another. The two spheres hover, touching, alongside
one another. In the *Logic,* in accordance with its thematics and
no doubt also under the pressure of the later Hegel's increasing
rigidity, external history is swallowed up in the inner historicity
of the exposition of the categories. But at least the exposition
almost never forgets intellectual history in the narrower sense.
When the *Logic* delimits itself from other views of the same subject matter, it always makes reference to the theses that have
been handed down as part of the history of philosophy. In obscure sections it is generally advisable to extrapolate such link-
ages. Earlier Hegelian texts, such as the *Differenzschrift* or the
Jena *Logic,* should be adduced. Often they offer programmatic
formulations of things the *Logic* will try to carry out, and they
allow themselves the references to the history of philosophy that
are later suppressed in the interests of the ideal of the movement of the concept. To be sure, a shadow of ambiguity lies across

this layer of Hegel's work as well. But just as the great systematic reflections feed on impulses from the historical, so the latter are influenced in their course by the systematic. They are seldom fully exhausted by the philosophical idea to which they allude. They are oriented more by objective interest than by an interest in so-called "encounters" with books. Even in the *Differenzschrift* one does not always know for certain what is directed against Reinhold, what against Fichte, and what already against Schelling, whose standpoint, while still officially defended, has already been transcended intellectually. Such questions could be resolved by Hegel philology if there were such a thing. Until that time interpretation in terms of the history of philosophy ought to strive for the same catholicity of interpretation as systematic interpretation.

Historical associations, moreover, are by no means the only ones that arise in connection with Hegel. Let me suggest at least one other dimension of associations. Hegel's dynamic is itself a dynamic of fixed and dynamic elements. This separates him irreconcilably from the kind of vitalist "flow" to which Dilthey's method dilutes him. The consequences of this for his structure should be explored. Much more invariance finds its way into the concept in motion than anyone who has too undialectical a conception of the notion of the dialectic itself would expect. However much the doctrine of the categories is negated in its details, Hegel's conception of an identity within the whole, of the subject-object, requires that doctrine. For all the richness of what Marx, in a musical metaphor, called Hegel's grotesque crag melody,[49] the number of his motifs is finite. However paradoxical it may be, the task of establishing a catalogue of the invariant elements in Hegel and working out their relationship to those that are in motion is an urgent one. It would serve understanding as well as provide a pedagogical aid, although of course it would do so only in undiminished consciousness of the one-sidedness that according to Hegel is itself untruth. The reading of Hegel must make a virtue of appropriation out of the necessity of the disturbing clatter about whose presence in classical music Richard Wagner made an analogous complaint. In the most difficult passages it is helpful to associate from one's knowledge of Hegel's invariants, which he certainly did not point out and which may be embedded in his work against his will, to the possible basis of the individual remark at hand. Often a comparison between the general motif and the specific wording supplies the meaning. The unorthodox overview of the whole without which one cannot do this requites Hegel for being unable to operate orthodoxly himself. Whereas Hegel, like free thought in general, is inconceivable without a playful element to which one owes the associations, the latter are only a partial moment. Their opposite pole is the exact wording. The second level of appropriation involves trying the associations out on the wording, eliminating those that contradict it, and leaving those that are in accordance with it and that illuminate the details. In addition to this kind of fruitfulness, the criterion for evaluating associations is that they are compatible not only with what is there but with the context as well. In these terms, reading Hegel is an experimental procedure: one allows possible interpretations to come to mind, proposes them, and compares them with the text and with what has already been reliably interpreted. Thought, which necessarily moves away from the text, from what is said, has to return to it and become condensed within it. John Dewey, a contemporary thinker who for all his positivism is closer to Hegel than their two alleged standpoints are to one another, called his philosophy "experimentalism." Something of this stance is appropriate for the reader of Hegel. At the current stage of Hegel's historical unfolding, such second-order empiricism would

bring out the latent positivistic moment contained, for all Hegel's invectives against narrow-minded reflective thought, in his
philosophy's stubborn insistence on what is. He who presumes
to seek spirit in the quintessence of what is thereby bows to the
latter more deeply than he admits. Hegel's ideal of reconstruc-
tion is not absolutely distinct from the scientific ideal: among the
unresolved contradictions in the Hegelian dialectic, this is perhaps the one richest in implications. Hegel provokes the experimental method, which is otherwise recommended only by pure
nominalists. To read him experimentally is to judge him by his
own criterion.

But what this says is that no reading of Hegel can do him
justice without criticizing him. The notion that critique is a second level erected on a foundation of understanding, an idea derived from pedagogical platitudes and authoritarian prejudice,
is in general false. Philosophy itself takes place within the permanent disjunction between the true and the false. Understanding takes place along with it and accordingly always also becomes,
in effect, a critique of what is to be understood when the process
of understanding compels a different judgment than the one
that is to be understood. It is not the worst reader who provides
the book with disrespectful notes in the margin. There is no need
to deny the pedagogical danger that in doing so students may
get involved in empty words and idle speculation and elevate
themselves above the matter at hand in narcissistic comfort, but
that has nothing to do with what is the case epistemologically. It
is up to the teacher to protect the interplay of understanding
and criticism from degenerating into pretentious emptiness. When
it comes to Hegel, a particularly high degree of such interplay
must be demanded. Indications about how to read him are necessarily immanent. They are aimed at helping to extract the objective substance from his texts instead of philosophizing about

his philosophy from the outside. There is no other way to get into contact with the matter at hand. The immanent approach need not fear the objection that it is without a perspective, mollusklike and relativistic. Ideas that have confidence in their own objectivity have to surrender *va banque,* without mental reservations, to the object in which they immerse themselves, even if that object is another idea; this is the insurance premium they pay for not being a system. Transcendent critique avoids from the outset the experience of what is other than its own consciousness. It was transcendent and not immanent critique that took up the standpoint against both the rigidity and the arbitrariness of which philosophy turned in equal measure. Transcendent critique sympathizes with authority in its very form, even before expressing any content; there is a moment of content to the form itself. The expression "as a . . ., I . . .," in which one can insert any orientation, from dialectical materialism to Protestantism, is symptomatic of that. Anyone who judges something that has been articulated and elaborated—art or philosophy—by presuppositions that do not hold within it is behaving in a reactionary manner, even when he swears by progressive slogans. In contrast, the claim Hegel makes for his immanent movement—that it is the truth—is not a position. To this extent that movement is intended to lead out beyond its pure immanence, although for its part the latter too has to begin within the limitations of a standpoint. He who entrusts himself to Hegel will be led to the threshold at which a decision must be made about Hegel's claim to truth. He becomes Hegel's critic by following him. From the point of view of understanding, the incomprehensible in Hegel is the scar left by identity-thinking. Hegel's dialectical philosophy gets into a dialectic it cannot account for and whose solution is beyond its omnipotence. Within the system, and in terms of the laws of the system, the truth of the nonidentical manifests itself as error, as unresolved, in the other sense of being unmastered, as the untruth of the system; and nothing that is untrue can be understood. Thus the incomprehensible explodes the system. For all his emphasis on negativity, division, and nonidentity, Hegel actually takes cognizance of that dimension only for the sake of identity, only as an instrument of identity. The nonidentities are heavily stressed, but not acknowledged, precisely because they are so charged with speculation. As if in a gigantic credit system, every individual piece is to be indebted to the other—nonidentical—and yet the whole is to be free of debt, identical. This is where the idealist dialectic commits its fallacy. It says, with pathos, nonidentity. Nonidentity is to be defined for its own sake, as something heterogeneous. But by defining it nonetheless, the dialectic imagines itself to have gone beyond nonidentity and to be assured of absolute identity. Certainly what is nonidentical and unknown becomes identical as well in being known; and in being comprehended, the nonconceptual becomes the concept of the nonidentical. But the nonidentical itself does not merely become a concept by virtue of such reflection; it remains the content of the concept, distinct from the concept. One cannot move from the logical movement of concepts to existence. According to Hegel there is a constitutive need for the nonidentical in order for concepts, identity, to come into being; just as conversely there is a need for the concept in order to become aware of the nonconceptual, the nonidentical. But Hegel violates his own concept of the dialectic, which should be defended against him, by not violating it, by closing it off and making it the supreme unity, free of contradiction. *Summum ius summa iniuria.* Through the sublation of the dialectic, reciprocity is restructured to become one-sidedness. Nor can one simply leap from reciprocity to the nonidentical; that would mean that dialectic had forgotten its understanding of universal mediation. But only by a Münchhausen trick, by pulling itself up by its own boot-straps, could it eliminate the moment that cannot be fully absorbed, a moment that is posited along with it. What causes the dialectic problems is the truth content that needs to be derived from it. The dialectic could be consistent only in sacrificing consistency by following its own logic to the end. These, and nothing less, are the stakes in understanding Hegel.

Notes

References to Hegel's works are noted as follows: the reference to the German edition cited by Adorno is given first, followed by the reference to the published English translation, if one has been used in the text. Where no reference to an English-language publication is given, the translation in the text is my own. Adorno cites the Jubiläumsausgabe of Hegel's works reissued under the editorship of Hermann Glockner and published by the Friedrich Frommann Verlag between 1927 and 1965. In these notes the following abbreviations have been used:

WW 1: Aufsätze aus dem kritischen Journal der Philosophie (und andere Schriften aus der Jenenser Zeit)

WW 2: Phänomenologie des Geistes

WW 3: Philosophische Propädeutik

WW 4: Wissenschaft der Logik, 1. Teil

WW 5: Wissenschaft der Logik, 2. Teil

WW 7: Grundlinien der Philosophie des Rechts

WW 8: System der Philosophie, I. Teil

WW 9: System der Philosophie, II. Teil

WW10: System der Philosophie, III. Teil

WW11: Vorlesungen über die Philosophie der Geschichte

WW12: Vorlesungen über die Aesthetik, I. Bd.

WW15: Vorlesungen über die Philosophie der Religion, I. Bd.

WW16: Vorlesungen über die Philosophie der Religion, 2. Bd.

WW17: Vorlesungen über die Geschichte der Philosophie, I. Bd.

WW18: Vorlesungen über die Geschichte der Philosophie, 2. Bd.

WW19: Vorlesungen über die Geschichte der Philosophie, 3. Bd.

For references to published English translations of Hegel's works, the following abbreviations have been used:

Difference: *The Difference between Fichte's and Schelling's System of Philosophy*, trans. and ed. W. Cerf and H. S. Harris (Albany, NY: State University of New York Press, 1977).

Phenomenology: *The Phenomenology of Spirit*, trans. A. V. Miller (Oxford: Oxford University Press, 1977).

Propaedeutic: *The Philosophical Propaedeutic*, trans. A. V. Miller (Oxford: Blackwell, 1986).

Logic: *The Science of Logic*, trans. A. V. Miller (London: George Allen & Unwin; New York: Humanities Press, 1969).

Right: *The Philosophy of Right*, trans. T. M. Knox (Oxford: Oxford University Press, 1942).

Logic/Encyclopedia I: *Logic: Part One of the Encyclopaedia of the Philosophical Sciences*, trans. William Wallace (Oxford: Oxford University Press, 1975).

Nature/Encyclopedia II: *Philosophy of Nature: Part Two of the Encylopaedia of the Philosophical Sciences*, trans. A. V. Miller (Oxford: Oxford University Press, 1970).

Mind/Encyclopedia III: *Philosophy of Mind: Part Three of the Encyclopaedia of the Philosophical Sciences*, trans. William Wallace and A. V. Miller (Oxford: Oxford University Press, 1971).

Philosophy of History: *Lectures on the Philosophy of History*, trans. J. Sibree (London: George Bell & Sons, 1894).

Aesthetics: *Hegel's Aesthetics*, trans. T. M. Knox, vol. 1 (Oxford: Oxford University Press, 1975).

Philosophy of Religion: *Lectures on the Philosophy of Religion,* trans. E. B. Speirs and J. B. Sanderson, in three volumes (New York: The Humanities Press, 1962).

History of Philosophy: *Lectures on the History of Philosophy,* trans. E. S. Haldane and Frances H. Simson (New York: The Humanities Press, 1955).

The translation of the German word *Begriff* has been consistently changed from "notion" to "concept" in quoted passages.

Introduction

1. These studies include Marcuse's *Hegel's Ontology and the Foundations of a Theory of Historicity,* his *Reason and Revolution: Hegel and the Rise of Social Theory,* his analyses of Marx's early writings, and his *Eros and Civilization: A Philosophical Inquiry into Freud;* Habermas's *Knowledge and Human Interests,* which deals with Kant, Hegel, Marx, Peirce, Dilthey, and Nietzsche, and his *Theory of Communicative Action,* which deals with Marx, Weber, Durkheim, Mead, Parsons, Adorno, Horkheimer, and Lukács; and Adorno's *Kierkegaard, Metacritique of Epistemology* (Husserl), *Jargon of Authenticity* (Heidegger), *Negative Dialectics* (Kant, Hegel, Heidegger), and *Hegel: Three Studies.*

2. This is the basis on which Fredric Jameson in his *Late Marxism: Adorno, or, the Persistence of the Dialectic,* has recently proposed Adorno as a model dialectical thinker for the 1990s and predicted a revival of an "unfamiliar materialist-mathematical" Hegel as well.

Aspects of Hegel's Philosophy

1. Hegel, WW 19, p. 611; *History of Philosophy* III, p. 479.

2. Ibid., p. 613; *History of Philosophy* III, p. 481 [translation altered].

3. Ibid., p. 615; *History of Philosophy* III, p. 483.

4. Richard Kroner, *Von Kant bis Hegel,* vol. 2 (Tübingen: Mohr, 1924), p. 279.

5. Cf. J. G. Fichte, *Science of Knowledge (Wissenschaftslehre),* trans. Peter Heath and John Lachs, first and second introductions (New York: Appleton-Century-Crofts, 1970).

6. Arthur Schopenhauer, *On the Basis of Morality,* trans. E. F. J. Payne (Indianapolis: Bobbs-Merrill, 1965), p. 63.

7. Hegel, WW 10, p. 305; *Mind/Encyclopedia* III, p. 187.

8. Karl Marx, *Early Writings*, trans. and ed. T. B. Bottomore (New York: Mc-Graw-Hill, 1964), p. 202.

9. Cf. Hegel, WW 4, p. 588f.; *Logic*, p. 472f.

10. Cf. the conclusion of the essay "Skoteinos," in this volume.

11. Hegel, WW 2, p. 30; *Phenomenology*, p. 15.

12. Ibid., p. 171; *Phenomenology*, p. 130.

13. Karl Marx, "Critique of the Gotha Program," in *The Marx-Engels Reader*, ed. Robert Tucker (New York: Norton, 1972), pp. 382–383.

14. Cf. Kroner, p. 404f.

15. Hegel, WW 2, p. 531; *Phenomenology*, p. 421.

16. Cf. Max Horkheimer and Theodor W. Adorno, *Dialectic of Enlightenment* (New York: Herder and Herder, 1972), pp. 25–26.

17. Hegel, WW 7, p. 319f.; *Right*, pars. 245 and 246, p. 151.

18. Ibid., p. 322f.; *Right*, par. 249. p. 152.

19. Ibid., p. 396; *Right*, par. 288, p. 189.

20. Hegel, WW 2, p. 23; *Phenomenology*, p. 10.

21. Hegel, WW 4, p. 87; *Logic*, p. 81.

22. Ibid., p. 87f.; *Logic*, p. 82.

23. Hegel, WW 8, p. 204; *Logic/Encyclopedia* I, p. 158.

24. Hegel, WW 4, p. 110; *Logic*, p. 99.

25. Ibid., p. 107; *Logic*, p. 97.

26. Hegel, WW 8, p. 91; *Logic/Encyclopedia* I, p. 53.

27. Ibid., p. 35.

28. Hegel, WW 2, p. 25; *Phenomenology*, pp. 11–12.

29. Ibid., p. 46; *Phenomenology*, p. 28.

30. Ibid., p. 22; *Phenomenology*, pp. 9–10.

31. Hegel, WW 10, p. 17; *Mind/Encyclopedia* III, p. 6.

32. Hegel, WW 8, p. 372; *Logic/Encyclopedia* I, p. 305.

33. Hegel, WW 4, p. 46; *Logic*, p. 50.

34. Hegel, WW 2, p. 38f.; *Phenomenology*, pp. 22–23.

35. Hegel, WW 7, p. 387f.; *Right*, par. 280, p. 184–185.

36. Cf. Kroner, p. 386.

37. Hegel, WW 2, p. 479; *Phenomenology*, pp. 379–380.

38. Kuno Fischer, *Hegels Leben, Werke und Lehre*, Part 1 (Heidelberg: C. Winter, 1901), p. 87; English in Walter Kaufmann, *Hegel: Reinterpretation, Texts, and Commentary* (Garden City, New York: Doubleday, 1965), p. 329.

The Experiential Content of Hegel's Philosophy

1. Martin Heidegger, *Hegel's Concept of Experience* (San Francisco: Harper & Row, 1970), p. 113.

2. Ibid., p. 120.

3. Hegel, WW 2, p. 613; *Phenomenology*, p. 487.

4. Ibid., p. 78; *Phenomenology*, p. 55.

5. Cf. this volume, pp. 9–10.

6. Hegel, WW 9, p. 58; *Nature/Encyclopedia* II, p. 19.

7. Hegel, WW 15, p. 174; *Philosophy of Religion* I, p. 162.

8. Hegel, WW 19, p. 283; *History of Philosophy* III, p. 176.

9. Hegel, WW 8, p. 50; *Logic/Encyclopedia* I, p. 12.

10. Ibid., p. 172; *Logic/Encyclopedia* I, p. 130.

11. Ibid., p. 181; *Logic/Encyclopedia* I, p. 138.

12. Cf. Hegel, WW 8, par. 213, p. 423f; cf. *Logic/Encyclopedia* I, par 213, p. 352f.

13. Hegel, WW 1, p. 54f; *Difference,* pp. 97–98.

14. Hegel, WW 12, p. 207; *Aesthetics,* p. 149.

15. Hegel, WW 17, p. 69; *History of Philosophy* I, p. 40.

16. Hegel, WW 8, p. 57; *Logic/Encyclopedia* I, p. 20.

17. Cf. Hegel, WW 19, p. 606; cf. *History of Philosophy* III, p. 473.

18. Hegel, WW 3, p. 125; *Propaedeutic,* p. 84.

19. Hegel, WW 18, p. 341.

20. Hegel, WW 8, p. 47; *Logic/Encyclopedia* I, p. 9.

21. Immanuel Kant, *The Critique of Pure Reason,* preface to the 2nd edition, trans. Norman Kemp-Smith (London: Macmillan, 1963), p. 29.

22. Hegel, WW 8, p. 36.

23. Cf. Hegel, WW 2, p. 46ff; cf. *Phenomenology,* p. 30.

24. Friedrich Nietzsche, *Aus der Zeit der Morgenröthe und der fröhlichen Wissenschaft 1880–1882, Gesammelte Werke,* Musarionsausgabe, vol. 11 (Munich: Musarion Verlag, 1924), p. 22.

25. Hegel, WW 8, p. 220; *Logic/Encyclopedia* I, p. 173.

26. Ibid., p. 173; *Logic/Encyclopedia* I, p. 130.

27. Hegel, WW 16, p. 309; *Philosophy of Religion* III, p. 101.

28. Hegel, WW 8, p. 423; *Logic/Encyclopedia* I, p. 353.

29. Hegel, WW 1, p. 527.

30. Cf. Hegel, WW 11, p. 49; *Philosophy of History,* p. 22.

31. Cf. Georg Lukács, *Realism in Our Time,* trans. John and Necke Mander (New York: Harper and Row, 1964); and Theodor W. Adorno, "Extorted Reconcilia-

tion: On Georg Lukács' *Realism in Our Time,*" in *Notes to Literature* I, trans. Shierry Weber Nicholsen (New York: Columbia University Press, 1991), p. 216ff.

32. Theodor W. Adorno, "From a Letter to Thomas Mann on His *Die Betrogene,*" in *Notes to Literature,* vol. 2, trans. Shierry Weber Nicholsen (New York: Columbia University Press, 1992), pp. 320–321.

Skoteinos

1. Hegel, WW 4, p. 493; *Logic,* p. 400.

2. Hegel, WW 1, p. 60; *Difference,* pp. 102–103.

3. Cf. this volume, pp. 50–51.

4. Hegel, WW 8, par. 212, addition p. 422; *Logic/Encyclopedia* I, pp. 351–352.

5. Cf. J. M. E. McTaggart, *A Commentary on Hegel's Logic* (Cambridge: Cambridge University Press, 1931).

6. Hegel, WW 7, par. 157, p. 236f.; *Right,* p. 110.

7. Cf. Hegel, WW 1, p. 56f; cf. *Difference,* pp. 99–100.

8. Hegel, WW 4, p. 488; *Logic,* p. 396.

9. René Descartes, *Principles of Philosophy,* trans. Valentine Rodger Miller and Reese P. Miller, (Dordrecht: Dr. Reidel, 1984), p. 20.

10. Descartes, *Oeuvres, Principia Philosophiae,* vol. 3 (Paris, 1905, first part), p. 21f.

11. Immanuel Kant, *The Critique of Pure Reason,* preface to the 2nd edition, trans. Norman Kemp-Smith (London: Macmillan, 1963), p. 373 (B415).

12. Descartes, "Discourse on Method," trans. by John Veitch, in *The Rationalists* (Garden City, NY: Doubleday, 1974), p. 63.

13. Ludwig Wittgenstein, *Tractatus Logico-Philosophicus* (New York: Harcourt Brace, 1922), p. 189.

14. Hegel, WW 17, p. 348; *History of Philosophy* I, pp. 281–282.

15. Cf. Edmund Husserl, *Ideas: General Introduction to Pure Phenomenology,* trans. W. R. Boyce Gibson (New York: Collier, 1962), p. 188.

16. Ibid., p. 185.

17. Ibid., p. 189.

18. Ibid.

19. Ibid., p. 190.

20. H. G. Hotho, *Vorstudien für Leben und Kunst* (Stuttgart and Tübingen, 1835), p. 386; English in Walter Kaufmann, *Hegel* (Garden City, NY: Doubleday, 1965), p. 351.

21. Cf. Friedrich Überweg, *Grundriss der Geschichte der Philosophie,* vol. 4, revised by T. K. Oesterreich (Berlin: Mittler, 1923), p. 87.

22. Hegel, WW 5, p. 5; *Logic,* p. 577.

23. Ibid., p. 13f; *Logic,* p. 583.

24. Hegel, WW 4, p. 536; *Logic,* p. 432.

25. Ibid., p. 658f; *Logic,* p. 526.

26. Hegel, WW 2, p. 619; *Phenomenology,* p. 492.

27. Hegel, WW 10, par. 411, p. 246f; *Mind/Encyclopedia* III, p. 147.

28. Hegel, WW 3, p. 211; *Propaedeutic,* p. 157.

29. Hegel, WW 5, p. 203; *Logic,* p. 729.

30. Hegel, WW 2, p. 390; *Phenomenology,* p. 308.

31. Ibid., p. 405; *Phenomenology,* p. 321.

32. Hotho, p. 384f; English in Kaufmann, *Hegel,* p. 351.

33. Hegel, WW 4, p. 87; *Logic,* p. 82.

34. Ibid., p. 665; *Logic,* p. 531.

35. Cf. Max Horkheimer and Theodor W. Adorno, *Dialectic of Enlightenment,* (New York: Herder and Herder, 1972), p. 25ff.

36. Hegel, WW 7, par 3, p. 43f; *Right,* pp. 16–17.

37. Gustav Rümelin, *Reden und Aufsätze* (Tübingen, 1875), p. 48f, quoted in Überweg, p. 77.

38. Hegel, WW 5, p. 328; *Logic,* p. 824.

39. Ibid., p. 240; *Logic,* p. 758.

40. Ibid., p. 240f; *Logic,* p. 758.

41. Ibid., p. 329; *Logic,* p. 825.

42. Ibid., p. 352f; *Logic,* p. 843.

43. Hegel, WW 7, par. 280, p. 387ff; *Right,* pp. 184, 288–289.

44. Hotho, p. 386f; English in Kaufmann, *Hegel,* pp. 351–352 (translation amended).

45. Hegel, WW 2, p. 44f; *Phenomenology,* pp. 27–28.

46. Cf. Hegel, WW 4, p. 665f and WW 5, p. 212; cf. *Logic,* pp. 531f and 736.

47. Hegel, WW 4, p. 552; *Logic,* pp. 444–445.

48. Hegel, WW 5, p. 343ff; *Logic,* pp. 836–838.

49. Cf. Karl Marx, *Die Frühschriften,* ed. Siegfried Landshut (Stuttgart: A. Kroner, 1953), p. 7.

Name Index

Studies in Contemporary German Social Thought

Thomas McCarthy, General Editor